ROME

HISTORY AND TREASURES OF AN ANCIENT CIVILIZATION

WHITE STAR PUBLISHERS

CONTENTS

INTRODUCTION
PAGE 10

CHRONOLOGY
PAGE 17

FROM THE BIRTH OF ROME
TO THE END OF THE REPUBLIC
PAGE 22

ASPECTS OF
CIVIC LIFE
PAGE 54

MAJOR EVENTS OF THE GREAT
MEDITERRANEAN EMPIRE
PAGE 86

THE LEGACY OF
ROMAN CIVILIZATION
PAGE 202

INDEX - BIBLIOGRAPHY
PAGE 204

1 - THE "BOCCA DELLA VERITÀ" (MOUTH OF TRUTH) IS A LARGE MASK IN MARBLE WHICH PORTRAYS A RIVER GOD.

2-3 - A BATTLE SCENE IS PORTRAYED ON THE FRONT OF THE LUDOVISI SARCOPHAGUS (AD 251) (NATIONAL ROMAN MUSEUM, ROME).

4-5 - THIS FRESCO IN THE MAIN HALL OF THE VILLA OF MYSTERIES SHOWS PREPARATIONS FOR AN INITIATION RITE.

6-7 - THE INSCRIBED COLUMNS DEDICATED TO THE CELEBRATED AUGUSTUS ARE IN THE TEMPLE IN THE CENTER OF THE LEPTIS MAGNA THEATER.

8 - THIS CAMEO IN ONYX WITH AN EAGLE AND THE CROWN OF VICTORY, BOTH SYMBOLS OF IMPERIAL ROME, DATE FROM THE AUGUSTINE ERA (27 BC-AD 14) (KUNSTHISTORISCHES MUSEUM, VIENNA).

TEXT
MARIA TERESA GUAITOLI

EDITORIAL DIRECTOR
VALERIA MANFERTO DE FABIANIS

COLLABORATING EDITORS
LAURA ACCOMAZZO
GIORGIO FERRERO
GIADA FRANCIA

GRAPHIC DESIGNER
PAOLA PIACCO

© 2006 White Star S.p.A.
Via Candido Sassone, 22/24
13100 Vercelli, Italy
www.whitestar.it

TRANSLATION TEXT: ANGELA MARIA ARNONE
TRANSLATION CAPTIONS: CORINNE COLETTE

All rights reserved. This book, or any portion thereof, may not be reproduced in any form without written permission of the publisher. White Star Publishers¹ is a registered trademark property of White Star S.p.A.

ISBN-10: 88-544-0147-1
ISBN-13: 978-88-544-0147-1

REPRINTS:
1 2 3 4 5 6   10 09 08 07 06

Color separation: Fotomec, Turin
Printed in Italy

INTRODUCTION

Roman civilization continues to arouse interest because of the important role it played in handing down values that even today are part of Europe's cultural heritage. The realization of Alexander the Great's dream of a magnificent empire (the diffusion of a Hellenistic civilization with its geographical horizon extending to a Mediterranean, or European, or even – and why not? – universal dimension) still awakens curiosity and admiration. Concrete traces of works completed by Rome are present and clearly visible to the eyes of all, whether the most famous monuments of Rome itself or public works scattered across Italian territory. Aqueducts, bridges, great temples or theaters (often used now as exhibition sites) are the most obvious traces Roman civilization has left, but there is also the underlying imprint, noticeable in the urban layout of towns that originated as colonies.

A glance at a blueprint of cities like Verona, Bologna, Aosta, and Brescia will reveal the traces of urban planning that Rome imposed in the late 2nd and early 1st centuries BC. The urban fabric of the Roman era subsequently became the underpinning for Medieval development: the main squares in countless Italian towns were once the Forum – the center of Roman public life – and many Christian churches are built over the foundations and mimic the layout of the civic building called the basilica.

Rome stood entirely apart in its aspiration to and atmosphere of greatness. The city's monuments, in the Late Republican age and particularly in the Imperial age, often included the most masterful and unsurpassed range of architectural typologies; for instance, Pompey's Theater, the Coliseum, and Trajan's Forum. The phenomenon of *imitatio urbis* (an imitation of Rome), which marked the great monumental construction periods in the provincial towns proves the extent to which the capital had served its purpose as an inexorable reference model, both in real life and in the mind's eye.

This reference to the *Urbs* (Rome) is also detectable in the provinces, the empire's "external" territories: in the West, from France to the Iberian peninsula, through Germany and in general, and across Central-Northern Europe as far as Great Britain; in Africa and in the East, where the monuments reminiscent of Roman dominion are a spectacular frame to the structures created by previous civilizations. Roman civilization's legacy is not only the settlements, the works of figurative art, the sculptures and paintings that adorned and decorated temples, porticoes and lavish private homes (now often on display in museums), but also in the cultural heritage of literature and the body of law and jurisprudence, still-living elements that constitute the bedrock of our own European civilization.

Nevertheless, Rome's greatness lies in the fact that it was not the passive heir to the Hellenistic world and to Alexander's empire. It successfully imposed a winning formula, in a unique synthesis that embraced all the many ancient cultures, successfully influencing the world for many centuries, applying a model that has yet to be equaled.

10 - THIS BRONZE EQUESTRIAN STATUE OF MARCUS AURELIUS, TODAY IN THE COURTYARD OF THE CAPITOLINE MUSEUMS, WAS UNTIL ONLY A FEW YEARS AGO IN THE CENTER OF THE PIAZZA OF THE CAMPIDOGLIO (ROME'S CITY HALL), WHICH TODAY HOLDS AN EXACT COPY OF IT.

11 - THIS VIEW OF THE CENTER OF ROME SHOWS WHAT REMAINS OF THE REPUBLICAN ROMAN FORUM, WITH THE COLISEUM IN THE BACKGROUND.

The great "scheme of history" that Rome achieved, but certainly did not originally plan, led to the development of an empire that united the East (the world then believed to be the successor to the great Graeco-Hellenistic civilization) and the West (a universe comprising many realities still considered "provincial," but with a great cultural and social substratum). Historians consider Rome's aptitude for integrating these two worlds within the panorama of her culture to be the secret of a great civilization.

Nonetheless, not just Rome, but the Roman world overall established itself as a archetype, or rather as the concrete expression of the Hellenistic *koiné* (common language), cherished by Alexander the Great. The process of Roman cultural expansion basically occurred in two stages. The first was that in which Rome established its power in the Etruscan-Italic world, which Roman civilization never really shrugged off, even in the production of its own forms of art and architecture. Once Rome had become the point of reference for all of ancient Italy's political, social and cultural activities, it began to compare itself with the great Mediterranean civilizations:

the Carthaginian and Graeco-Hellenistic, from which it inherited and developed a particular and unique "lifestyle." In the second stage of its evolution, with the establishment of the empire that at the end of the 1st century BC replaced the Republican regime, Rome came into contact with other "provincial" realities, located on the outskirts of what was the known world at that time, for instance Continental Europe's territories and is western provinces. Rome's "common language" was the result of a cultural policy that absorbed hints, suggestions and revisitations, and extended to all fields of knowledge in civic and political life, the figurative arts and architecture. This language, filtered through the unique traits of each Italic and provincial situation, led to the creation of a civilization that was able to evolve for eight centuries. It was a culture that bridged the gap between the Hellenistic world, rooted in the Mediterranean and Eastern provinces, and the Western world, belonging more to Continental Europe. Undeniably, it was the culture that gave birth to modern Europe and the Western World through its cultural role that was operating even in the Medieval universe.

12 - A DETAIL OF A MOSAIC PAVEMENT, FROM SABRATHA, WHICH PORTRAYS THE HEAD OF AN AFRICAN FELINE IN A ROUNDEL. (TRIPOLI MUSEUM).

13 - THE THREE PRAETORIAN GUARDS ARE FROM THE HONORARY ARCH DEDICATED TO CLAUDIUS (AD 51). THEY ARE BIZARRELY WEARING GREEK-ILLYRIAN TYPE CRESTED HELMETS (THE

The focus of this text is first of all the narration of historic events that makes it possible to outline the development of the empire. Secondly, it is an analysis of surviving evidence of building policies and art production in Rome's Republican and Imperial phases. From the Renaissance onwards, artists and scholars focused their admiration on Rome: the monuments and relics of the ancient world's "capital of all capitals" became style models to imitate, or the target of collectors from the era's great aristocratic families. The city of Rome was also an essential stopover for journeys of discovery that poets and literati of the 1700s and 1800s made in Italy, reflecting the particular interest the city fueled, not only for its ruins but also for the objects produced by the Roman world's provincial sphere.

The book explores a series of phases, repeating its journey from the center (Rome) to the outskirts (the provinces), which analyze Rome from its genesis. First the foundation of Rome, as a proto-urban center at the hub of an accumulation of populations culturally and economically "dominated" by the influence of the Etruscans and Italiots (the inhabitants of Magna Graecia).

Legend, history and archaeology interweave in this reconstruction of Rome's origins, revised on the basis of the most recent archaeological findings from the Palatine Hill, which reveal new details about the era of the monarchy founded by Romulus. Previous, accepted historical interpretations about Rome' archaic phase are completely overturned. After Rome's conquest and domination of central-southern Italy, the city's rise was relentless. Following Rome's encounter with the Hellenistic world, a source of inspiration for those cultural models revisited through the traditional motifs of the culture of the Middle-Italic period,

the foundations were laid for a world that was culturally independent and unique, especially as far as economy, law, jurisprudence and functional architecture were concerned.

With the "construction" of the Mediterranean empire (the world conceived at that time as the fulcrum of civilization), it was possible to observe the progressive involvement of the populations (those of Central-Western Europe: Celts, Rhaetians, Germans, Thracians, etc.) that would contribute to the creation of a new, original language. Its expression would be mainly through art forms and language and it would become the basis for cultural, figurative and artistic expressions that modern Europe would then inherit from the Carolingian Middle Ages.

Historians have pinpointed the end of Marcus Antoninus' rule (AD 161) as the chronological marker separating the apogee of Roman civilization from the substantial change that was a prelude to its decline. The reign of Commodus (AD 180-192) heralded a crisis of the consolidated "values" that were part of the cultural legacy in the Eastern-Hellenistic stamp. This "crisis," with its cultural and political nuances, was to spawn not only a new language, but also a new historical vision. With the advent of the new emperor, Constantine (AD 307-337), the way opened irrevocably for a new and "different" Christian universe, cutting a path to the Middle Ages, the cradle of our current Western civilization. The shift in perspective – first from the Mediterranean to Rome, then to the provincial world and lastly to Europe – was a historic process that is the keystone of our cultural substratum. It cannot be overlooked, bearing in mind that the Roman world and its cultural universe survived external political and military pressure for about 800 years, and succeeded in spreading models that are still admired and imitated by contemporary society.

HADRIAN'S WALL

16

BRITANNIA

ATLANTIC
OCEAN

LONDINIUM

LOWER
GERMANY

GALLIA
BELGICA

GALLIA
LUGDUNENSIS

TREVIRORUM   UPPER
GERMANY

LUTETIA

AUGUSTODUNUM

RHAETIA

GALLIA
AQUITANIA

LUGDUNUM

AUGUSTA
RAURICA

NORICUM

BURDIGALA

AOSTA

GALLIA
NARBONENSIS

PANNONIA

DACIA

LUSITANIA

NARBO

ITALY

DALMATIA

UPPER
MESIA

LOWER MESIA

AUGUSTA
EMERITA

HISPANIA
TERRACONENSIS

CORSICA

ROME

THRACIA

ADRIANOPOLIS

TARRAGONA

OSTIA

HISPANIA
BAETICA

CORDOBA

SARDINIA

POMPEII

MACEDONIA

MAURITANIA
TINGITANA

CESAREA
MAZACA

EPIRUS

PERGAMON

CAESARIAN
MAURITANIA

SICILY

CARTHAGE

EPHESUS

ATHENS

CORINTH   MILETUS

SYRACUSE

ACAIA

TIMGAD

BULLA
REGIA

DOUGGA

CRETE

PROCONSULAR AFRICA

MEDITERRANEAN SEA

SABRATHA

CYRENAICA

LEPTIS MAGNA

CYRENE

GHIRZA

16-17 - The map shows the expanse
and organization of the Roman
Empire in its provinces during the
period of its maximum expansion in
the early 2nd century AD.

18-19 - The upper level of the Arch of
Constantine (312-315 BC) has statues
and reliefs from other eras: the
statue of the Getae prisoner, formerly
in Trajan's Forum, and the Aurelian

reliefs (AD 173) with scenes of captives
(condemned by a barbarian chieftain)
and the rex datus (the presentation of
tribute to the barbarians by the king).

20-21 - The detail of the mosaic of the
Centaurs under attack by tigers and
leopards used to decorated the
cryptoporticus of Hadrian's Villa in
Tivoli (AD 130-138) (Staatliche Museen,
Antikensammlung, Berlin).

MONARCHICAL ERA
(about 753-470 BC)

The founding of Rome laid the basis for a radical change in the political layout the peoples of Latium had known until then. They had been organized into villages and not according to an urban pattern and, now, Rome imposed itself as the center of its territory from which it dominated all commercial and political events. This dominion was beset by power struggles which sometimes even extended to the borders of Etruscan domination. After a period of the Etruscan hegemony of the Tarquinian dynasty, Rome definitely freed itself from Etruscan influence in the early 5th century BC and established a regime along republican-aristocratic lines. As a consequence, the arts, too, were strongly influenced by the inflow of Etruscan tenets and Greek models which began to appear on the horizon of Roman culture.

REPUBLICAN ERA
(450-23 BC)

During the 1st Republic (until 264 BC), Rome consolidated its power within the Italic world, subjugated peoples including the Samnites and the Lucanians and codified its internal politics. With the subjection of Southern Italy, strongly under Greek influence and part of the so-called Magna Graecia, Rome began to assimilate the values of Greek civilization and to open up to the Mediterranean world. The battle with Carthage (from 264 to 146 BC) definitely sanctioned Rome's expansion throughout the Mediterranean while the Illyrian and Macedonian Wars - and those in the Orient and in Africa against ruling dynasties throughout most of the Mediterranean descended from Alexander the Great - saw the beginning of the first system for domination of the provinces. Rome's internal politics, in the meantime, began to see crisis because of a conflict related to social reform between the two social classes: the patricians and the plebeians. This situation culminated in civil war (83-80 BC) and, as a result, saw the restructuring of the social order by the dictator, Sulla. From this time onward, Rome's politics alternated between "dictators" and triumvirates until C. Julius Caesar expanded Rome's dominion by subjugating the Gauls and created a sort of autocratic government. His assassination, and the civil war which followed as a consequence, signaled the end of the Republic with the rise to power of Octavian and the creation of the principate between 27 and 23 BC. Throughout this entire period, the Greek-Hellenistic model dominated not only the arts and city-planning but also custom.

IMPERIAL ERA
(23 BC-AD 285)

The Imperial Period was marked by the rule of various dynasties: notably Iulius-Claudius and Flavius. After a period under various adoptive emperors (Nerva, Trajan, Hadrian, Antoninus Pius and Marcus Aurelius AD 96-180) dynastic succession resumes with Commodo (AD 180-193), and, lastly, with the Severans. In the first phase, we see Rome's maximum expansion: Rome has now become a "universal empire" marked by the Hellenistic inheritance of Alexander the Great, and a government that gained ever greater stability. The government of the provinces was divided between the Eastern and Western territories and extended from Europe to the Mediterranean countries, Northern Africa, Asia Minor and part of the Arabian peninsula. The Roman model, especially its urban one, was imposed throughout the dominion and superseded even pre-existing situations. Political crisis began in AD 180 and was linked to the problem of control of the empire's borders, which were threatened by the barbarians. The consequent crisis of stability, due to the army's growing mistrust of its rulers and to the spread of Asian cults, led to a period of confusion beset with struggles among various generals: it terminated only with the advent of Diocletian.

BYZANTINE ERA
(285-476 AD)

The constitution of the tetrarch launched the decline of the Roman Empire also because of its loss of bordering territories and, on the political-ethical level, due to the spread of Christianity. The advent of Constantine brought about the definite division between the two parts of the Roman Empire: the East and the West, but while the former was destined for longer life, the latter fell under the barbarians in 476 BC.

BLACK
SEA

BYSANTIUM

BITHYNIA AND
PONTUS

GALATIA   CAPPADOCIA

ASIA

APHRODISIAS

LYCIA   CILICIA

ASPENDOS

RHODES

SYRIA

PALMYRA

CYPRUS

BAALBEK

CESAREA
MARITIME

JUDEA   JERASH

JERUSALEM

ALEXANDRIA

PETRA

ARABIA
PETREA

EGYPT

RED
SEA

CHRONOLOGY

HISTORY AND TREASURES OF AN ANCIENT CIVILIZATION

FROM THE BIRTH OF ROME
TO THE END OF THE REPUBLIC

THE FOUNDING OF ROME

The foundation of Rome (traditionally 753 BC) was a momentous event that influenced not only the settlement of Latium itself, but also the entire Ancient World, not to mention the later role the city was to play as the epicenter of Medieval Europe. Rome initiated the construction of an architecture bound to precise political-institutional significance, and which characterized the urban planning and life of all Imperial centers. In point of fact, the urban expansion of Rome and its military conquests led to the gradual diffusion of the Roman urban model, first throughout Italy and subsequently in the territories embraced by the empire.

Public architecture, of course, but also private buildings, aligned with the cultural models proposed by elite (with emperor and aristocracy in the front line); this was especially so in those elements of daily life that celebrated the private sphere (monumental tombs, the *domus*, banquet furnishings, etc). This complex system combined the public and private dimension, leading to the birth of what historians, archaeologists and art historians all call the "shared language," i.e., a set of values in different cultural contexts that bridged the gap from Classical civilization to Medieval Europe.

Historians explore many themes reflected by ancient historical tradition to justify the establishment of Rome's power, but the most realistic may perhaps be seen as the city's fortunate geographical position, near an important ford across the River Tiber. Since the Bronze Age, this position channeled local trade traffic toward the area of the future Forum Boarium, at the foot of the Capitoline Hill. Here there was a river port with a goods sorting and salt storage emporium (salt was especially precious, in particular for inland shepherds).

Extensive data that prove that the Forum Boarium district was a privileged part of archaic Rome, compared to the political and economic power hubs that were to evolve in the city in later years. From the start it was precisely the geographical position of Rome, a city of Latin *ethnos*, that hallmarked it as a frontier town between the territories occupied by Latin peoples (defined as *Latium vetus*), the northern areas of Etruria, Southern Italy's Greek colonies, and the Italic peoples of the Apennines. Its role as a commercial emporium ensured that the city was open-minded and pervious to the most diverse cultural and ethnic influences, making it the center of fervid activity and the ideal location for developing supreme dominion first over the Italic world and later over the Mediterranean.

This is primarily why the study of ancient Roman history, itself an era of learning, is fundamental for understanding the role and significance of structures that went on to form the empire, exploring how they evolved and how they were classified, models that were to be handed down and perpetuated for the next eight centuries. Then, returning to what was to become Rome's glowing future, it is also useful to examine the circumstances that turned this group of shacks on the Tiber (initially not so dissimilar to others scattered across Latium and Italic territory) into the heart of an empire.

Rome's enormous capability for civilization lay not so much in its imposing its urban-planning, artistic or political model on the populations it gradually conquered (a sort of before-the-term "globalization") but rather in adapting solutions and parameters to existing realties it encountered, case by case. For instance, this occurred with the development of a primary symbiosis in the areas already permeated by the historic substratum and culture of the Graeco-Hellenistic world (Southern Italy and the Eastern provinces), or with the acculturization of local populations in the areas where no such deep-rooted tradition existed.

Rome itself was the major player in a process of overlapping Greek cultural models with ancient Italic traditions. Yet again, in this case, however, the hinging performed by craftsmen and central power in urban-planning and building policy meant that the indigenous traditional element and the external element, acknowledged as more eminent, fused into an original synthesis, capable of re-elaborating and preserving the peculiarities of both primary cultures.

23 - THE BUST OF "CAPITOLINE BRUTUS" COMBINES MOTIFS OF ETRUSCAN PAINTING AND GREEK PORTRAITURE (CAPITOLINE MUSEUMS, ROME).

24 - THE RELIEF FROM THE 1ST CENTURY BC REFERS TO THE *SULCUS PRIMIGENIUS*, A RITE FOR THE FOUNDING OF A CITY (NATIONAL ARCHAEOLOGICAL MUSEUM, AQUILEIA).

25 - The bronze statue of the
Capitoline She-wolf (5th century
BC), feeding Romulus and Remus
with her milk, is the symbol of Rome
(Capitoline Museums, Rome)

The foundation of Rome, the first step on its journey to becoming one of history's greatest empires, was fostered by a number of fortunate conditions, completely unlike any enjoyed by the other towns that existed on Latium territory at the time. The new settlement's position was first-rate and, above all, differed from the usual village and *agger* (rampart) layout, so it immediately emerged as an open city, hallmarked by its Tiberina Island river port, which allowed it to control trade and all goods arriving for distribution to inland populations. As occurred with many Latium sites, it is likely that the first stable settlement of Rome's seven hills (the Palatine, Aventine, Quirinal, Viminal, Capitoline, Esquiline, and Coelian) comprised a series of small villages clinging to vestiges of Late Bronze Age culture. This phenomenon, called "synoecism" (the amalgamation of smaller villages into larger units) is documented by the remains of huts and items of material culture, brought to light on the Palatine and surrounding hills, and is an extensively documented system in Italian protohistory, especially for Villanovan-Etruscan cultural scenarios. The swampy nature of the flat land seems to have impeded – at least initially – any stable residential settlement on the plains, to the point that the valley where the city's forum eventually arose was used for a time as a burial ground.

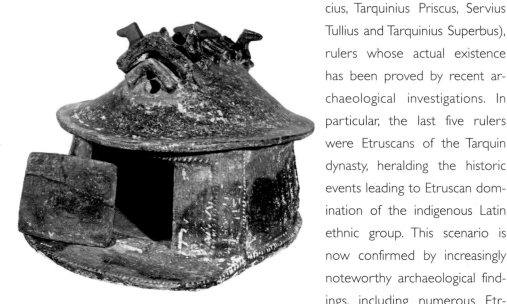

The reasons behind Rome's great economic and commercial development were evident to the city's early historians, who emphasized just how much of the city's fortune was attributable to its specific geographic location, along the lower course of the Tiber, near an important ford. Originally it was a huge market and from ancient times this was an evident feature that made the city a point of reference for inland populations. The emporium actually developed along a bridge (the *pons Sublicius*) that spanned the Tiber and connected Rome to Etruria and the coast, as well as being the point of arrival of the roads in from Latium's southern towns. This was how the ancient city managed to control important trade routes like Via Campana and Via Salaria (this latter's name reveals its role as the commercial road for salt brought from the flats at the Tiber's mouth). In fact, for Latium's inland shepherd population salt was of fundamental importance for cheese-making and preserving meat.

From the time of its origins Rome's location between Latium and Etruria allowed it to absorb a wide variety of ethnic influences (with consequent cultural interaction) with the Sabines, the Etruscans and the Greeks. Concurrently, a second and only superficially contradictory peculiarity, namely Rome's "frontier" position compared to the more important inland Latium towns, made a decisive contribution to its social, cultural and political growth.

Tradition dates Rome's foundation to 753 BC, with an initial period of monarchy under the "legendary" Seven Kings. After its founder Romulus and the Sabine king Titus Tatius, the successors were: Numa Pompilius, Tullus Hostilius, Ancus Marcius, Tarquinius Priscus, Servius Tullius and Tarquinius Superbus), rulers whose actual existence has been proved by recent archaeological investigations. In particular, the last five rulers were Etruscans of the Tarquin dynasty, heralding the historic events leading to Etruscan domination of the indigenous Latin ethnic group. This scenario is now confirmed by increasingly noteworthy archaeological findings, including numerous Etruscan inscriptions brought to light around the Velabrum, Forum Boarium and the Capitoline area, which would later be known as *vicus Tuscus* (the Tuscan district). The dynasty, which boasted Greek origins (it is said that Tarquinius Priscus' father was Demaratus, the famous Corinthian descendent of the noble Bacchiades family), successfully established a policy of innovation with a program focused chiefly on politics and building, aiming not only to create public works, but also to separate political and lay power from religious supremacy; a factor that was to be the underpinning of the future role of Rome in the known world.

In fact, during the Tarquin dynasty's reign, Rome became a great city: wealthy and powerful, very much in contrast to the austere image of a pastoral economy that Sallust (c. 86-35/4 BC) and several other later historians have presented. If the truth be told, the Tarquins are to be thanked for reclamation of the Forum area and for the installation of a massive drainage channel, called the *Cloaca Maxima*. The Forum was also the location of several buildings that were to be most representative of Rome's future public image: the *Comitium*, housing political and jurisdictional functions, and the *tabernae*, housing business enterprises. Consequently, the Forum area came to be the city's preferred political site, with neighboring religious and trade sectors. Moreover, new markets and traffic areas were developed for commercial needs, not to mention enhancement of the traditional Forum Boarium and Forum Holitorium, whereas construction of the great Jupiter Optimus Maximus temple on the Capitoline stands as the most prestigious example of religious architecture from the monarchical period.

Despite the foresight of the Tarquins, responsible for creation of an urban fabric, as well as foundation of institutions and positions that became the underpinning of Republic and Empire, the Monarchy (whose style of government had changed, in any case, mimicking Greek and Eastern tyranny) was, however, abandoned (by tradition in 509 BC) in favor of the Republic. This change led to heavy contrasts developing between Roman society's two dominant components: the plebians (*plebs*) and the patricians.

This is the historic watershed of the city's growth that separates two eras. The first, the period of the Monarchy, was linked to the urban planning policies of Tarquinius Priscus (616-579 BC) and Servius Tullius (578-535 BC), with definition of the city's major urban structures (political, military, financial, religious) and the establishment of four urban territorial tribes that survived intact until Augustus (27 BC-AD 14) ordered new subdivisions. After the watershed, in the First Republican age (5th century BC), a bipolar urban system emerged, reflecting political strife between the plebs and the patricians. During the era of the Tarquins, the social order was completely reorganized and the entire population was divided into four *tribus*, in turn subdivided into 10 sections (*curiae*) of equestrians and "people" (*plebs*). This system was based on a patriarchal system of allied groups of relatives, lineages and families, from whom the king recruited his councilors (*senatus*) and army leaders, almost all belonging to the equestrian class (*equites*). The conflict between the plebs and the patricians, which evolved from the early days of the Republic, had its factions located on the Aventine, the heart of political power, on one hand, and at the Forum Boarium, the beating heart of business and economic life, on the other.

26 - THE ETRUSCAN HUT-SHAPED FUNERARY URN IN TERRACOTTA FROM VULCI COPIES THE STRUCTURE OF THE ANCIENT LATIUM DWELLINGS WITH A ROUND LAYOUT, A SLOPING ROOF AND WITH ACROTERIAL DECORATIONS (VILLA GIULIA NATIONAL MUSEUM, ROME).

27 - THE STATUE OF APOLLO WAS PART OF A MOLDED CLAY GROUP WHICH DECORATED THE COLUMEN OF THE TEMPLE OF PORTONACCIO IN VEIO (LATE 6TH CENTURY BC), AND WAS MADE BY FAMOUS ETRUSCAN ARTISTS WHO LATER ALSO WORKED IN ROME (VILLA GIULIA NATIONAL MUSEUM, ROME).

In 335 BC, about 150 years after the fall of the Monarchy and establishment of the Republic, Rome minted its first coin, significantly with a ship's bow as its emblem, testifying to the trade links that the city was forging with the rest of the known world. Only the word *pecunia* (derived from *pecus*, or livestock assets), used to label the "new object," retained any trace of the Archaic era's main form of barter and trade

As far as external alliances and military security were concerned, however, Rome found itself in a central position, among the Italic populations (Oscans to the north and Samnites to the south), and the Etruscans and Greeks. Against this backdrop of ongoing conflict and pressure to conquer new territories, especially after the Greek defeat of the Etruscans in the naval battle of Cumae (474 BC), marking the end of their domination of the peninsula, Rome managed to create a federal system that guaranteed massive military potential on which to rely, and simultaneously constructed its own domestic, Republican political organization: the two factors were to prove fundamental for establishing its supremacy worldwide. In the army there was actually a revolution that consequently affected the political scenario: battle tactics relied on the extensive use of heavy infantry – mainly peasants – in a compact array. So the cavalry, despite a supremacy acquired due to its victories, was ousted and the position of the plebs was reinforced, although they continued to be excluded from top military command. Politically, the first consequence was the establishment of a sort of judiciary to defend the interests of the plebs, known as their "tribuneship." Later, in about the mid-4th century BC, supreme power of command (*imperium*) was entrusted to two consuls and a praetor, the latter with juridical functions. Nevertheless, as the 4th century BC drew to a close, the plebs slowly acquired the right to hold important army ranks and were even admitted to the Senate, as well as being given access to sacerdotal appointments.

From the 3rd to the 2nd century BC, however, the rise of Rome was attributable to its Italian territorial expansion rather than its internal politics. The decline of Etruscan hegemony, the peace stipulated with the Latin League (sealed by the pact known as the *foedus Cassianum* in 493 BC) and above all the victory of the Italic Confederation in the Samnite Wars (which had continued at intervals from 326 to 272 BC), gave Rome control over central Italy, and brought it into direct contact with the Hellenistic-Mediterranean world of Magna Graecia. Following the victory in 272 BC over Pyrrhus, king of Epirus, Rome – at the request of the citizens of Taranto – took control of a vast territory extending from the Marches and taking in Campania and Apulia. Above all, for Rome this expansion meant the assured availability of a large military contingent. This was not yet a professional army: it comprised recruits from among Romans and colonials governed by Roman law, with the financial wherewithal to procure their own equipment; it was nonetheless, a far cry from the mercenary armies serving the Hellenistic powers of that time.

28 - THE EFFIGY OF PYRRHUS, KING OF EPIRUS, IS HERE PORTRAYED IN MARBLE (NATIONAL ARCHAEOLOGICAL MUSEUM, NAPLES).

29 - THE THREE COINS ABOVE PORTRAY THE PROW OF A SHIP. BELOW, WE SEE AN EXAMPLE FROM THE 3RD CENTURY BC, THE PERIOD WHEN MONEY WAS FIRST COINED IN ROME (BRITISH MUSEUM, LONDON).

Political control of conquered territories was achieved by instituting colonies (under Roman and under Latin law) and *municipia* (towns). The new colonies were given "characteristic" structures, imported from the capital and intended to perpetuate Rome's image throughout history. Rome was the blueprint for a number of urban-planning elements that were recovered and served as emblems of the brand-new colonial settlements: fortified walls (to delimit urban from rural space); the *Comitium* (seat of municipal worship and a bond of loyalty between Rome and towns of the Roman world, often replacing a temple dedicated to Jupiter); the *Curia* and the Forum with their annexes, in particular the basilica, which were seats of local administrative power but also warrantors of the new urban community's independent yet centralized vocation.

The various forms of colonial derivations that envisaged institutional and functional forms designed to reflect dependency on the city of Rome were also reflected in the organization of urban layouts and structures. Colonies under Roman law, ruled directly by Rome, were small in size and inhabited by Roman citizens, and were conceived for military control, mainly of the coast. It was no coincidence that the urban fabric mimicked the original, square-plan military camp, or *castrum*, installed at the junction between two main roads (the north-south *cardo maximus*, and the east-west *decumanus*

maximus), which can be clearly seen in the oldest example of this type of urban structure: Ostia, founded in 380 BC. On the other hand, colonies governed by Latin law were in some way dependent on the Latin League, and citizens enjoyed special rights from Rome; generally, the populations numbered several thousand settlers and their function, as well as their vocation, was to establish agricultural colonies on the territory. This is also reflected in the urban layout, influenced by the Greek colonial orthogonal street plan, a system that brought a network of quarters (elongated rectangular blocks called *insulae*) and streets (a division known as *per strigas*).

A new type of urban layout arose in the 2nd century BC, following Rome's colonization of Northern Italy and especially of the Po Valley: rectangular blocks were replaced with squares, whose sides were two *actus* in length, equal to 236 ft (72 m). This urban layout was applied to Verona, Pavia, Como, Piacenza, Cremona, Parma, Modena and Bologna, with Aosta, Turin and Fano following suit in the subsequent Augustan period.

Urban design seems to have been experimented with in Cisalpine territory (i.e., south of the Alps), but it may be that this phenomenon simply reflected centuriate territorial organization, whereby farmland was divided up into "hundreds" applying a regular intersecting axis model, using the standard base module.

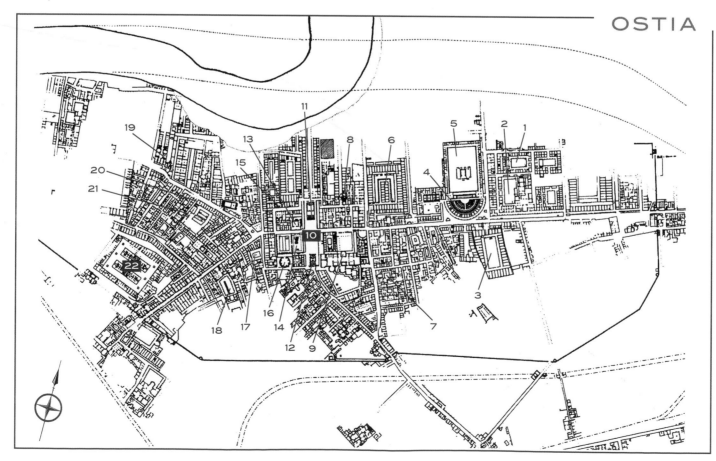

OSTIA

30-31 - THE ANCIENT PORT OF ROME AT THE MOUTH OF THE TIBER, WAS OSTIA, AND ITS URBAN LAYOUT CAN STILL BE SEEN; IN THE FOREFRONT WE SEE THE *CAPITOLIUM* AND NEXT TO IT, THE REMAINS OF THE *CURIA* AND THE *HORREA EPAGATHIANA*.

Rome's real opportunity to extend its supremacy beyond Italic territorial boundaries came with the Punic Wars against Carthage, the first in 264-241 and the second in 218-201 BC. The wars began after conflicts in Sicily between the so-called Mamertin (Oscan mercenaries serving Agathocles, tyrant of Syracuse) and Hieron, the city's new ruler. In reality, the Punic Wars were fought by both sides, Romans and Carthaginians, each with the intention of extending its dominion over Sicily, as well as to Corsica, Sardinia and much of the Iberian peninsula. Whilst Rome was still fending off Hannibal and the Carthaginian armies, a new conflict arose to the east, to fight off Illyrian pirates and to counter Carthage's alliance with King Philip V of Macedonia, who intended to expand his Greek territories, an event which would be especially damaging for the kingdoms of Rhodes and Pergamum, allies of Rome.

Macedonia and Greece's demotion to Roman provinces after Rome's victories in the Macedonian Wars (200-197 BC and 171-168 BC), the destruction of Corinth in 146 BC, victory in the Syrian War (193-188 BC) against one of the Diadochian dynasties (those set up by the Diadochi or "Companions," as Alexander the Great's successors were called), and success against the Seleucids all led to provincial reorganization of Eastern territories, already in part allied with Rome. Moreover, in 133 BC, Rome inherited the kingdom of

Pergamum, as ordered by Attalus III in his will, and in 74 BC, that of Bithynia, bequeathed by Nicomedes III. Contact with kingdoms that carried Greek and Hellenistic intellectual legacies was to have a significant effect on Rome, both culturally and from the domestic policy aspect. In fact, Rome found itself governing huge territories (juridically transformed into *provinciae*, administered by *pro consules* and *pro praetors*) in which different cultural and political scenarios dominated, far more intense than those of the Italic and Latin world.

Direct control of the Eastern provinces channeled great wealth to Rome, establishing activities linked to trade and to the management of contacts with the province, especially by the aristocratic classes and the *nobilitas*. The new nature of great power destabilized the *latifundium*-based agricultural organization (i.e., based on large agricultural estates) that was the traditional bedrock of the Roman economy, and gave rise to strong social revolt among the *populares* (ordinary people), following the attempt at agrarian reform proposed by Tiberius Gracchus (133 BC), and then by his brother, Gaius (123 BC). Moreover, the Social War with the Italic tribes, laying claim to Roman citizenship (90-88 BC), destabilized the entire Republican system: this was when figures began to emerge from the *nobilitas* (the aristocracy), who used personal prestige and wealth to underpin their political campaigns.

32 - THIS SILVER COIN SHOWS A BARCA, A MEMBER OF HANNIBAL'S FAMILY, ON ONE SIDE AND AN ELEPHANT ON THE OTHER, TESTIFYING TO POWER WITHIN THE CARTHAGINIAN POLITICAL ORDER (BRITISH MUSEUM, LONDON).

33 - THIS BRONZE BUST VERY PROBABLY PORTRAYS A VICTOR OF THE SECOND PUNIC WAR (218-201 BC), PUBLIUS CORNELIUS SCIPIO AFRICANUS (NATIONAL ARCHAEOLOGICAL MUSEUM, NAPLES).

This trend also played an important role in architecture and art history, since the major characters in this contest used political construction or culture as targeted propaganda to assist their scaling of the power ladder. The first to enter this arena were Marius and Sulla, between 88 and 82 BC: the former led the *populares*, in particular supporting distribution of land to war veterans and concession of citizenship to the Italic *socii* (allies). Sulla stood with the *optimates* (the aristocrats) seeking to re-establish the Senate's failing supremacy, even resorting to lengthy proscription lists and confiscation of assets from supporters of the opposing faction.

Following Sulla's death (78 BC), the consuls Pompey and Crassus sought to promote a reform of the Republican order, but together they became Rome's new political protagonists. Pompey established himself on the military front, empowered by his suppression of piracy in 67 BC and his military victories against King Mithridates of Pontus shortly thereafter, which assured Rome control of the province of Syria. On his return to Rome, Pompey had to deal with domestic circumstances that opposed his suggested reorganization of the Eastern provinces, as well as his demands for land grants for his veterans. The existing power crisis was resolved by the arrival of one of Roman history's most famous figures: Caius Julius Caesar. He was called upon to act as guarantor and invited to join a triumvirate that included Pompey and Crassus, becoming consul in 59 BC. The alliance between Pompey (Rome's most powerful figure), Crassus (its richest) and Caesar (its most politically-mind-ed) was the event that finally dealt the deathblow to the ailing Republic. Following the conquest of Illyria and Gaul, with Rome extending its dominion as far as the Rhine and Britain, acquired through the concession of exceptional authority to Caesar, his Senate detractors began to accuse him of illegal behavior.

When Crassus was killed at the battle of Carrhae (53 BC) during his Parthian campaign, Caesar was forced into a direct confrontation with Pompey, the third member of the triumvirate; at the same time the Senate refused to extend Caesar's governorship of Gaul. Civil war broke out and shifted from Italy to the provinces: first Spain and then the East. Thanks to his loyal army, Caesar obtained the final victory, at Pharsalus in 48 BC: Pompey fled to Egypt, where he was traitorously slain by the henchmen of Cleopatra's brother, Ptolemy. Under the pretext of avenging his former rival, but actually to squash Pompey's Republican following, Caesar went as far as Africa, vanquishing the last of Pompey's supporters at Thapsus (46 BC), eliminating those in flight in Spain, at Munda (45 BC). Military and political successes notwithstanding, the fear of a new form of government that might diminish the power of the Senate, led to Caesar's murder on the Ides (the 15th) of March, 44 BC.

Yet the political agenda for a renewal of the Republic that had been sought, first indirectly by Pompey, then by Caesar, was subsequently implemented by the political program of the first great emperor: Octavian Augustus (27 BC-AD 14).

35 - This bust of Caius Julius Caesar shows him as a young man and doesn't show his proverbial baldness; it is probably from the Augustine era, based on the way his hair is arranged, typical for that period (Kunsthistorisches Museum, Vienna).

CITY-PLANNING ASPECTS OF ROME AND ITS COLONIES

36 LEFT - THIS MODEL IS OF
A LATIUM RESIDENCE, LIKE
THOSE OF THE PALATINE
(MUSEUM OF ROMAN
CIVILIZATION, ROME).

36 RIGHT - THESE HUTS
WERE MODELED AFTER
THE SO-CALLED "HUT-LIKE"
FUNERARY URNS (VATICAN
MUSEUMS, ROME).

How did the structure of Rome evolve against this backdrop of historic events and, above all, what models did it hand down to its provincial empire? We might start by looking at Archaic Rome, which grew within the boundaries (*pomerium*) mapped out by Romulus, establishing the limits of the city and of urban territory. Two decades of excavations here have cast light on ancient Rome's earliest architecture and on its ancient legend. There is little doubt now that the actual foundation date coincides with that handed down by tradition: the second half of the 8th century BC, the era of the wall unearthed on the Palatine slopes, which endorses an evident dividing line between an embryonic urban settlement and a real town. Archaeological research also dates the oldest royal palace or *Regia*, inside the sanctuary of Vesta, to this period, as well as the original priestesses' house, on the opposite side of the *Regia*. The palace has a monumental structure, although the construction technique is no different from that normally used for huts: support struts for clay walls, and roofed with branches. An entrance supported by huge wooden posts leads into a central room with a bench running along the walls, probably used as seating during ceremonies or banquets. Moreover, the luxurious 8th-century BC banqueting ceramics, brought to light in a basement storeroom, confirmed the theory that this was the prestigious seat of the first kings.

Romulus may not have lived here (sources indicate his residence as the Palatine), but his successors certainly did,

moving the royal residence to the vicinity of the Forum, where Vesta and Lares were worshipped, and which from that time on became the center of Roman life. The priestesses' house (*domus*), on the other hand, was an oval building with roof support shaft holes, hearths, cooking surfaces, and cereal containers. The building was sited exactly opposite the entrance of the temple where the sacred flame burned. It is known, of course, that the priestesses of Vesta (goddess of the sacred flame for both home and city, derived from the corresponding Greek divinity, *Hestía*) were subject to the sovereign's direct authority, and only he could live in the temple. The establishment of a sanctuary connected to the king's residence confirmed the birth of Rome as a city-state, and recognized the ideological nature of this location as a sacred and political mainstay.

During the First Republic, political friction between the patricians and the plebs also found expression in architectural installations and definition of areas selected as centers of power. One example is the colossal sanctuary dedicated to the Jupiter, Juno and Minerva triad, commissioned by the patricians and built on the Capitoline Hill, and the other temple, found on the Aventine and dedicated to Diana, commissioned by the plebs, possibly in response to the Capitoline colossus. The Jupiter temple on the Capitoline Hill (said to have been ordered by the Tarquins in about 580 BC) is a *sine postico* peripteral type (i.e., with only three sides enclosed by the peristyle, and a wall at the far side) with a double row of columns in the pronaos (the portico). The internal cella has three rooms: Jupiter's statue is in the center flanked by the other two divinities. The Capitoline temple, whose triple-cella construction served as a model for other temples, was still in the traditional Tuscan architectural style inherited from the Etruscans. This detail is also quite evident in the terracotta building decorations, using a quadriga as an acroterium on the apex of the roof, said by Pliny to have been produced by the workshop of the Veiian artist, Vulca.

In the Republican period, the capital's future evolution focused on two aspects: commercial enterprise, which might be seen as a "plebeian" vocation, and the civic, religious and political ambience, at the Forum-Capitoline complex. Architecturally, in fact, these segments attracted the interest of opposing classes right from the early days, with heated competition to build temples and sanctuaries dedicated to patron divinities. Thus temples to Hercules, protector of *negotiatores*, and to *Mater Matuta* and Portunus were built in the Forum Boarium, linked to divinities of Greek origin, but also to gods protecting traders in the Etruscan *emporion* at Pyrgi.

For its part, the new Republican aristocratic regime unveiled a temple to Saturn on the Capitoline Hill, where the senatorial class later chose to locate the Roman public treasury. Other monuments that also had practical functions were erected as urban monuments and symbols: the Comitium (a square, terraced space, emulating the Greek *ekklesiasteria*), to host public assemblies and the activities of the new judiciary, and the Curia, where the Senate met. The entire Forum was refurbished to accentuate its lay and religious nature; for instance, legendary sites like the Volcanal (an ancient statue) or the Niger Lapis (the Black Stone), a model of public space resembling the Greek *agorà* type. Subsequently, Furius Camillus ordered the Concordia temple to be dedicated to a commemoration of patrician-plebeian reconciliation, decisive confirmation of the Forum's symbolic function as the site where a power equilibrium had been achieved.

Another typical episode involves Republican Rome's second district: the Forum Boarium, also linked to the trade and plebeian sector. Following the destruction of the *Mater Matuta* and *Fortuna* temples, ideologically identified with Monarchical Rome, two new places of worship were built, where the plebs would meet in *concilium plebes* (the assembly of the plebs). It was no coincidence that the two temples were dedicated to Mercury, the patron divinity of trade (495 BC), and to the trio of Ceres, Liber and Libera (496 BC). A number of factors underscore the importance of this institution: first, the fact that the three divinities were the equivalent of the Greek divinities Demeter, Dionysus and Kore, widely worshipped in Southern Italy and Sicily, with strong popular associations. Secondly, despite the outward appearance of the temple, in the usual Etruscan mold, with wooden trabeation (according to Vitruvius), the cella's interior decoration of terracotta reliefs and slabs, was entrusted to Greek workers (Pliny says they were Damophilos and Gorgasos, two *plastae*). Lastly, the more explicitly political (and controversial) reason: the temple was built as the reply to and antagonist of the patrician temple dedicated to the Capitoline triad.

Architecturally speaking, the Forum Boarium temples have an Etruscan structure, which Vitruvius later christened the Tuscanic order: tall podium, distanced intercolumniation, extensive use of wood both for columns and roof, and polychromic terracotta trabeation decoration, in the Etruscan tradition. In point of fact, remains of several terracotta antefixes testify to the presence of a group of workers from Caere (Cerveteri), as early as the late 6th century BC. This site subsequently hired Veiian craftsmen, as in the above example of Vulca, the craftsman of the Capitoline triad temple decoration.

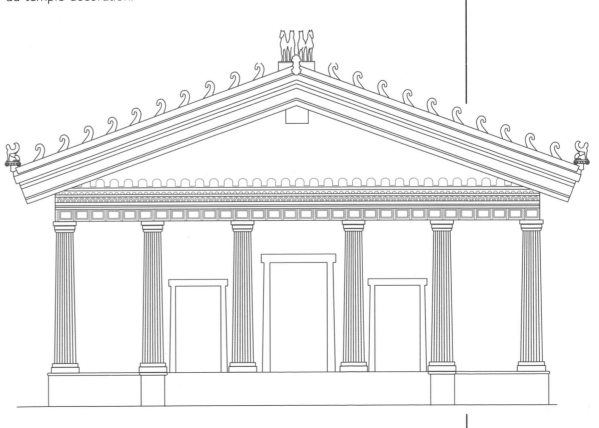

38-39 - From the Pompeii Forum,
we see the remains of the temple,
with a six-pillared front portico on
the podium, dedicated to Jupiter,
and the *Capitolium*, which closes
the city square.

A significant event occurred – one that was generally considered to mark the onset of the Hellenization phenomenon that affected Roman culture – with the assimilation of the canons of Greek art that began in 212 BC. This was the year when M. Claudius Marcellus captured Syracuse, an event which the historian Livy defined as the "*primum initium mirandi Graecarum artium opera*" – "the first marveling at the works of Greek art" (*Ab Urbe condita* XXV, 40, 1-3). This new Hellenization trend overwhelmed all sectors of Roman culture, and naturally also expressed the political-ideological discord between the old guard of aristocrats (the most vociferous of whom was Cato the Elder) who advocated safeguarding the austere customs of the past, and the new classes (like the Scipio family) that were more farsighted in terms of political resolutions and cultural growth in a broader sense.

Hellenization surged forward noticeably in the 2nd century BC and at the same time, following the Second Punic War, great works were commenced to make the city worthy of its new leadership of the other Italic populations and dependent colonies, a role which resulted from Rome's defeat of Carthage. First, the Romans initiated a series of public works: roads, aqueducts, and *horrea* (warehouses). However, the great innovation, which allowed monumental buildings to be erected, was the masons' introduction of a new material, *opus caementicium* (a mixture of mortar and pozzolana), invented in Campania, where builders used it extensively. Several types of structure first built in this region soon became extremely popular throughout the Roman world: in particular, public baths, first built in Capua in 216 BC, followed by those of Teano, and then the baths in the forum in Pompeii, built during the period of the Gracchi brothers (130s-120s BC). During this time, all Roman and Latin colonies also adopted the public structure of a forum with a temple, including the tall podium, and normally dedicated to the Capitoline triad.

39 - THIS FRESCO COMES FROM THE PRAEDIA OF IULIA FELIX, ONE OF THE LARGE PRIVATE HOMES NORTH OF THE POMPEII'S AMPHITHEATER; IT PORTRAYS THIS CAMPANIAN CITY'S FORUM, WITH EQUESTRIAN STATUES STANDING IN FRONT OF THE PORTICOES.

Application of the Greek model emerged chiefly in architecture, although initially it was an adaptation of existing models to forms deriving from the Hellenistic world. A fine example is the so-called temple of Hercules, on the acropolis at Cori, with its tetrastyle (four front columns, with fluting and a smooth Doric frieze), and Doric structure, but in conglomerate, and set on a tall podium.

The use of marble was actually still limited at this time, at least in Rome itself, with the exception of a temple still visible today. This temple was built in the Forum Boarium in the late 2nd century BC following the granting of a concession for the use of public ground, and was dedicated to *Hercules custos* by its chief sponsor, a Tiburtine merchant named M. Octavius Herennius. This circular building is in Pentelic marble, and the outer perimeter has twenty Corinthian columns, on a terraced *crepidoma* (base), with foundations in tufa from the Grotta Oscura quarries. The structure's importance lies in its full assimilation of the Greek model, both for the circular layout (a homage to the *tholoi*-type schema) and for the marble façade. It is also true that in that same period architectural orders began to include use of the Corinthian capital, which gradually ousted the traditional Tuscanic and Doric capital, and became completely established by the time of Augustus.

40 - IN THE NECROPOLIS NORTH OF GHIRZA, IN LIBYA, ARE SOME MONUMENTAL TOMBS FROM THE 3RD CENTURY AD. TOMB C HAS COLUMNS WITH CORINTHIAN TOPS OVER WHICH ARE SMALL ARCHES WITH FLORAL DECORATIONS IN ACCORDANCE TO ORIENTAL ARCHITECTURAL CUSTOM.

41 - A COLUMN TOP FROM THE TEMPLE OF HERCULES (OR VESTA) IN THE FORUM BOARIUM SHOWS THE CORINTHIAN INFLUENCE SEEN IN ITS BASKET OF ACANTHUS LEAVES. THIS TEMPLE (ABOUT 142 BC) WAS ONE OF THE FEW WITH A MARBLE CELLA AND PERISTYLE (ROMAN FORUM).

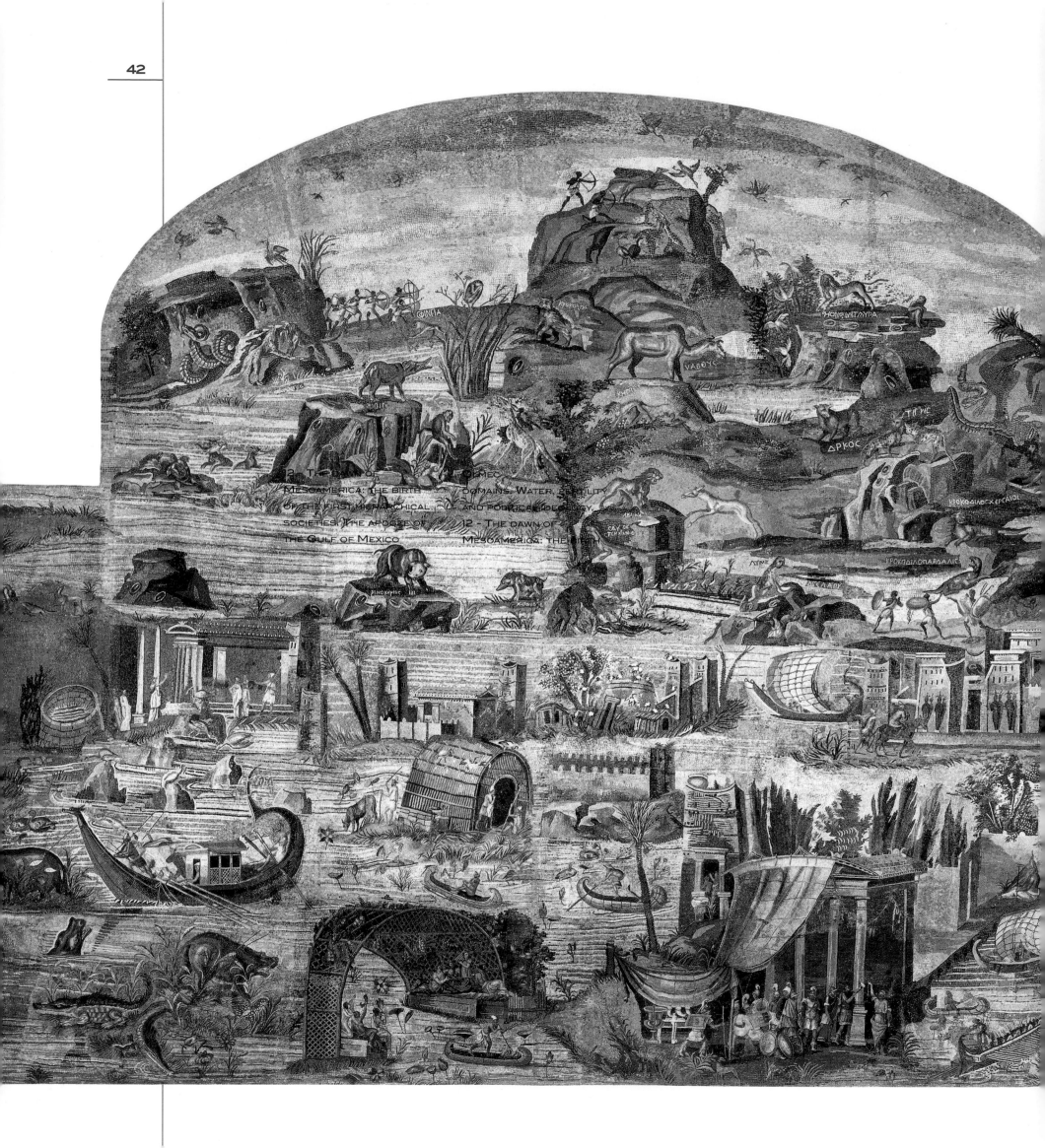

In Latium, within a scenario of the Italic world's trade domination of the Mediterranean basin largely through monopolies of oil, wine and similar commodities, each community initiated its own program of public and (chiefly) religious building. In this sense, the Fortuna Primigenia sanctuary at Praeneste (Palestrina) is undoubtedly a great expression of Republican architecture (a blend of Hellenistic and Italic styles), as is the sanctuary of Hercules Victor at Tivoli. At Palestrina, the temple is set against a striking backdrop (built on mighty substructions) connected by ramps and cadenced by exedras. The actual, round or *monopteros* (with only a single ring of columns) sanctuary stands at the top of the so-called Cortina Terrace, with a triple portico, joined to a cavea-type theater.

In Rome, the same architectural plan found in Pompey's theater with annexed temple of Venus, dated between 55 and 52 BC, whereas the temple at Palestrina is presumed to be of a phase between the late 2nd century BC and the Sullan period (105-80 BC). The complex soars upwards — dominating the habitat and connected to the Forum by a series of ramps — and is certainly the legacy of Greek town planning. Its inspiration can be identified in the prospect designed for Pericles' Athenian Acropolis (440s-430s BC), a design subsequently perfected and adopted for other sanctuaries, up to the version found in Pergamum, the Attalid dynasty's Hellenistic-style capital. From the fourth terrace up, linear and curvilinear motifs alternate in a succession of exedras (open porticoes) and vaulted structures, which nonetheless retain straight trabeation (rows of horizontal beams), with a series of Ionic, Doric, Doric frieze and Italic capital columns. The sculpted and dynamic appearance of the complex is also due to the use of *opus caementicium* (concrete) certainly more ductile than marble, lending

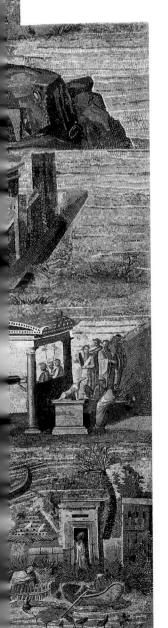

itself better to installation on the steeply-sloping terrain.

The Praeneste Museum, housed in a 1600s palazzo in Palestrina whose façade exploits the curving line of the upper hemicycle, is now home to the mosaics that decorated the temple. A famous Nilotic scene mosaic, originally found in the so-called apsidated chamber to the east of the basilica, expresses a pictorial penchant stimulated by Alexandrine realism, a genre linked to the scientific spirit of classification inspiring Alexandria's *Mouseion* Library (although in actual fact, the style is Iranian, later passing to the genre the Greeks called *paradeisos* (pool complex). On the west, the basilica is balanced by the "Cave of Destiny" (Antro delle Sorti), whose floor is paved with a mosaic depicting fish, thus also adopting the naturalistic theme so dear to the tastes of the Late Republic. Many of Republican Rome's *villae* (country seats) also had at least one room with this type of decorative motif, used not only as a naturalistic pattern for the flooring of *piscinae* (swimming-baths or fish tanks), but also frequently found as decoration of garden walls, a famous example being the Villa of Livia, at Prima Porta.

The temple of the Victorious Hercules at Tivoli, despite a floorplan resembling that of Palestrina, built on extensive substructions with the temple erected at the rear of the triple-arcade terrace, shows more linear, simple and geometrical solutions, nor is the cavea element quite as practical as that of the Praeneste sanctuary.

These buildings, in a Latium context, were heavily influenced by the Greek models, especially by two different artistic currents: the so-called "Pergamene Baroque" in the former, and a return to more contained Classic forms as far as Tivoli is concerned. The dichotomy is further reflected across the era's entire artistic production.

42 - THE NILOTIC MOSAIC OF THE TEMPLE OF FORTUNA PRIMIGENIA IN PRAENESTE SYNTHETICALLY UNITES SCENES OF THIS KIND TO ALEXANDRIAN REALISM (ABOUT 80 BC) (ARCHAEOLOGICAL MUSEUM, PALESTRINA).

43 - THE BIRD'S-EYE VIEW OF THE FORTUNA PRIMIGENIA TEMPLE COMPLEX AT PRAENESTE (82-70 BC) HIGHLIGHTS THE VARIOUS TERRACED LEVELS AND THE HALF-CIRCLE THEATER STRUCTURE WHICH HELD THE TEMPLE.

On the subject of ambition, Pompey and Caesar's subsequent building policy shifted its focus to the Campus Martius area, with the erection of two important architectural structures: the theater and the quadriporticus. The marble theater, the first in Rome of such a size and in resilient material, required a massive architectural and economic commitment. The quadriporticus, successor of a museum archetype of the ancient world, the Hellenistic *kepos*, for exhibiting works of art (almost a precursor of the Renaissance gallery), on the other hand, was a place for conversation and meditation.

This operation of Pompey's was not merely political, it was mainly cultural, aiming to uproot old *res publica* traditions and foster another genre of state organism, a prelude to the Empire. From 54 BC Caesar also began to engage in large-scale construction but, in opposition to Pompey, and with a haughty demagogic intent, he promoted the building of a marble *porticus* (gallery), called the Saepta Iulia, to be used for public elections. At the same time, Caesar initiated the building of a monumental complex, intended to be the greatest expression of celebration of his dynasty, in the style of the Hellenistic monarchs, using as a pretext the overcrowding of the Roman Forum. The result was the Forum Iulium, inaugurated in 46 BC, where he proposed to shift Rome's political nerve center. His *Lex de Urbe augenda*, an audacious building program, probably entrusted to a Greek architect, was never implemented and was set aside (for obvious reasons of political opportunism) by his successor, Augustus. The agenda envisaged the usual demagogic provision to increase dwellings for the people, but also the construction of a flamboyant theater, more monumental than that of Pompey, paying homage to the models of Pergamum, as well as the upheaval of Rome's city center, deviating the course of the Tiber so as to create an urban area reaching as far as the Campus Vaticanus, to concentrate the city's attention on the cult of his own *gens*, representing the new order.

44 - THE MODEL SHOWS POMPEY'S THEATER WITH THE TEMPLE OF THE VICTORIOUS VENUS AT THE CENTER-TOP OF THE *CAVEA* AND PORTICOES BEHIND THE SCENE (MUSEUM OF ROMAN CIVILIZATION, ROME).

45 - CAESAR'S FORUM INCLUDED THE TEMPLE OF *VENUS GENETRIX*, PROTECTOR OF THE *GENS IULIA*, IN MARBLE; IT SHOWED GREEK INFLUENCE, WITH ITS LARGE "SHOPS" (*TABERNAE*) IN LIMESTONE AND BRICK ON THE SIDE.

Now to return to Rome. In the early 1st century BC, in the period dominated by the soldier-politician Sulla, a new type of relationship arose between patrons and builders of great architectural works. What is more, Graeco-Oriental influence was cast aside so it was then possible to formulate a new type of urban planning policy that focused on the elevation of Roman genius and creativity in service to the demands of monumentalization in what was becoming the *caput mundi* (capital of the world). This new urban planning policy operated in the realm of public works; private construction continued to lack a precise city plan. There was, at that time, a huge, often impecunious population arriving from the countryside, increasing the need for new residential quarters that habitually developed at the fringes of popular districts, without application of any safety regulations. Since ground space was at a premium, the idea of building upwards developed, and produced the first example of *insulae*, the typical popular dwellings of the Imperial era, forebears of modern apartment blocks. Sulla's most ambitious city-planning project was, however, the creation of a majestic architectural backdrop, called the *Tabularium*, on the Capitoline Hill's southeastern slopes, later becoming the state archive, and forging a link with the Forum. This monument is especially important as it combines two innovative factors in Roman architecture: the extensive use of brick, and the round arch and vault.

46 top - This stone relief portrays a Roman city in perspective. the large buildings of the *insulae* are within its walls (Museum of Roman Civilization, Rome).

46-47 and 47 top - The models of the residential buildings (*insulae*) testify to the presence of apartment-style living even in ancient times (Museum of Roman Civilization, Rome).

Roman figurative language comprises many interwoven elements. In the Republican period main the inspiration came from the form and material preferred by the Etruscan-Italic artistic cultural tradition. Later contact with the *poleis* of Magna Graecia (and, more generally, with Greek masterpieces, as well as with Hellenic craftsman circulating in the Mediterranean basin), infiltrated Roman creative expression, which simply accommodated its ideological aspirations to these artistic forms. In this respect, Roman art continued to be characteristically utilitarian and didactic, imprinted with simple, immediate symbolism, serving political power and representing the *virtutes*, first of the magistrates then of the emperor, to eulogize the power of Rome.

Two artistic genres, both with strong political valence, evolved at this time, and were the most original of Roman art production: these were the honorary statue and the portrait. The origins of the portrait genre date back to the *imagines maiorum*, death masks made for various family members, carried and displayed on the hearse in a sort of triumphal ceremony for each new funeral (Polybius, *Histories*, VI, 53-54). This custom explains why Roman portraiture was attributed with aspects of authenticity and resemblance of the deceased that are in no way proven, not least of all because the primary function of the *imagines maiorum* was purely political, celebrating the glories of the lineage (*gens*), but simultaneously bound to the various religious values expressed by the ancestral cult.

From the 3rd century BC, the number of portraits produced grew disproportionately, particularly in the Late Republic (1st century BC), when the so-called *homines novi* (the new men) appeared on the political scene. These were people whose families had no political background, and rising to roles as top magistrates they needed to "construct" a family tree as an endorsement and confirmation of the power they had acquired. The best known example of this sense is the famed statue known as the *Togato Barberini* (the toga-clad Roman aristocrat), who had himself portrayed with busts of the only two ancestors, probably his father and his grandfather, to have achieved significant appointments and offices, therefore important figures in the political arena. So these are not true likenesses of physiognomic features, but simply power status expressions

The portrait genre also developed as terracotta *ex-votos*, enjoying popularity especially in the 4th and 3rd centuries BC, proving that the head was privileged above the rest of the body. This principle was contrary to Greek custom, which would find it totally unacceptable to separate the two parts of the anatomy.

The most famous artwork in the field of Roman portraiture is certainly the so-called *Capitoline Brutus*, a bronze head (possibly originally part of a statue), datable late 4th-early 3rd century BC, because two elements resemble other examples of the same period: the first is the physical resemblance to the profile of Velthur Velcha, painted on a wall of the *Tomba degli Scudi* ("Tomb of the Shields"; 350-325 BC) at Tarquinia; the second is the strong iconographic influence of contemporary Greek portraiture.

48 - THE STATUE KNOWN AS *TOGATO BARBERINI* (LATE 1ST CENTURY BC) IS A GOOD EXAMPLE OF THE POPULARITY OF PORTRAITURE IN ROMAN FIGURATIVE ART (CAPITOLINE MUSEUMS, ROME).

49 - THE *CAPITOLINE BRUTUS* WAS NAMED FOR HIS PRESUMED RESEMBLANCE TO THE CONSUL, BRUTUS, THE FOUNDER OF THE ROMAN REPUBLIC (CAPITOLINE MUSEUMS, ROME).

Political events led to another new genre: "triumphal painting," deriving from the custom of carrying the *tabulae triumphales* in processions to celebrate triumphant generals. The *tabulae* were then left on public display in official porticoes or buildings, to celebrate the patron's prestige or serve as political propaganda.

This usage evolved to produce what is defined as the archetype of historical painting (which preceded technical narrative of historic observation), the famous fresco in one of the Esquiline tombs. The fresco is indicated as the first example of historic triumphal painting, traditionally attributed, although not completely proven, to Fabius Pictor, al-

ready identified as the artist of the *aedes Salutis* paintings (303 BC).

This trend for historic illustration was flanked, particularly in the decoration of Roman dwellings, by the genre that reflected a preference for Hellenistic painting that illustrated episodes from the *Odyssey*. One fine example is the series of frescoes in a house on the Esquiline, datable 50-40 BC. Also of the Late Republican era is another private *domus*, known as the House of the Grifi, as well as the Farnesina house, which show a type of wall decoration resembling what was later called the "Second Pompeian style," in other words, *trompe-l'oeil* architectures painted on the walls, to create a sense of greater space.

As the Late Republic drew to a close there were also several types of sculpture that partly reflected Greek art, but also partly inherited historic realism. Mainly literary sources have handed down the names of craftsmen from Greece, or of Greek origin, working in Rome. The most important and versatile was certainly Pasiteles, whose pupil Stephanos is known to have sculpted the so-called Albani Athlete, a copy after the severe style of Greek art (late 6th-early 5th century BC), to which it pays homage. Then there was Arkesilas, a sculptor of Doric origin, author of the religious statue, commissioned by Caesar, installed in the Venus Genetrix temple.

Apart from statues, the field of sculpture also includes two other types of production: reliefs and portraits. The most famous relief monument, combining "mixed" features of Greek art and what was on the brink of being defined as Roman art, is the so-called Altar of Domitius Ahenobarbus, in part displayed in the Louvre, and in part in Munich's Glyptothek Museum. The Altar, whose date and interpretation are quite controversial, comprises a combination of relief slabs in different styles. One slab is a purely decorative Hellenistic relief depicting the marine *thiasos* (the cortège of Amphitrite and Poseidon). The second slab is considered a Roman relief, however, and its *lustratio* scene and *suovetaurilia* – the classic Roman religious sacrifice whose name came from the initials of the offering: pig (*sus*), sheep (*ovis*), bull (*taurus*) already reveal descriptive tendencies. On the basis of some historical motifs, the second slab can be dated about 107 BC, preceding the reforms Marius initiated. The Altar's interest lies in the Hellenistic-style mythological motif, combined with the realistic "Roman-type" depiction, a code found in many commemorative monuments of subsequent eras, the best example being the *Ara Pacis Augustae*.

The Forum's *basilica Aemilia* frieze is part of the same artistic trend, attributable to the early decades of 1st century BC, and is a historic illustration of episodes from the life of Romulus, Rome's legendary founder.

50 TOP LEFT - THIS FRESCO FRAGMENT (EARLY 3RD CENTURY, BC) IS FROM A TOMB IN THE NECROPOLIS ON THE ESQUILINE HILL AND IT SHOWS, ON THREE LEVELS, AN HISTORICAL SCENE RELATED TO THE SAMNITE WARS AND REFLECTS THE INFLUENCE OF THE ARTIST FABIUS PICTOR'S PAINTING.

50 TOP RIGHT - THE PAINTINGS IN THE HOUSE OF THE GRIFI ON THE PALATINE HILL (120-110 BC) ARE EXAMPLES OF THE SO-CALLED 2ND STYLE (ARCHITECTURAL) WHICH DEPICTS FAUX ARCHITECTURE.

50-51 - THIS PLATE BELONGS TO THE SO-CALLED ALTAR OF DOMITIUS AHENOBARBUS, AND ILLUSTRATES A *LUSTRUM CENSORIO* OR SACRIFICIAL SCENE TO HONOR MARS (THE LOUVRE MUSEUM, PARIS).

Alongside the marble sculpture, clay artworks were also still being produced in this period, used in particular for the decoration of temples, and were even more a derivation of Etruscan heritage. The survival of this technique, in any case, suggests precise political motivation, since it evokes archaic purity and simplicity (actually "invented" by members of the senatorial aristocracy as mere propagandistic motifs) to thwart *luxuria asiatica*, the predilection for Greek art products and models, created precisely, on the other hand, by the *homines novi*, members of the *equites* and new emerging classes.

There are also two trends to be seen in Late Republican portraiture: a Hellenizing vogue, of which the most famous and important example is the Tivoli statue of the "general," and the so-called analytical realism trend, identified in a famous portrait of Pompey the Great.

So, even in Rome's reproduction and imitation of Greek prototypes, the main styles of Hellenic art are evident, in particular that linked to Classicism (the Neo-Attic style) and that linked, conversely, to productions of the era subsequent to Alexander the Great (known as Neo-Hellenism). However, within the Roman world artists began to adapt and transform these styles, and initial resemblance was subsequently re-elaborated, influenced by countless components (Etruscan, Italic, but also "popular" or plebeian), especially in the narrative-stylistic context, contributing to Roman art's liberation from the Greek "prototype," in particular in artistic expressions found in the Imperial age and in the so-called "provincial" scenario.

52 - POMPEY THE GREAT IS HERE SEEN IN ONE OF HIS MOST FAMOUS PORTRAITS (60-50 BC) ANTICIPATING THE CLASSICAL STYLE TO BECOME POPULAR IN THE AUGUSTAN ERA (NY CARLSBERG GLYPTOTHEK, COPENHAGEN).

53 - AN EXAMPLE OF A "HEROIC STATUE" WHICH UNITES TWO STYLES, HELLENISTIC AND ROMAN; HERE, WE SEE A GENERAL, FROM THE HERCULES TEMPLE IN TIVOLI, SCULPTED DURING THE MITHRIDATIC WARS (FIRST HALF OF THE 1ST CENTURY, BC) (NATIONAL ROMAN MUSEUM, ROME).

2

ASPECTS OF CIVIC LIFE

The territory dominated by Rome had two distinguishing factors acting as "bond" and catalyst: religion and military organization. These factors contributed, among other things, to the diffusion and circulation of many aspects of Roman civilization. This meant not just culture, but also the more immediate issues of daily life, like trade, and in turn, distribution of objects that were part of the material culture.

Roman religion had specific characteristics that were closely bound to rituals, but required no precise act of faith. Moreover, religion was indissolubly linked to a social element, whether that element was the city, the family, or the military unit. Traditionally, ritual rules of worship were said to have been established by the legendary kings Romulus and Numa Pompilius, but subsequently redrafted by the magistrates. These rules were applicable to three aspects of daily life: definition of spaces, sacrifices to divinities, and prophecies. Naturally, the last of these three was influenced by the augural ritual, practiced by Etruscan religion, whereas Greek religion influenced the choice of divinities in the Roman pantheon. The most important of the rites regarded the definition of space for the foundation of a new city, which involved tracing out a furrow to delimit the settlement's outer walls, definition of the *pomerium*, a more extensive perimeter, beyond the walls, held to be sacred and inviolable. Finally, the augurs arrived to "liberate" chosen spaces from any evil influences. Several public spaces – including those for the actual *templa* (temples or sanctuaries) – were also "inaugurated" in a precise ritual that took into account cardinal compass points, and that was how civil and community activities were "consecrated."

Similarly, the calendar was organized to incorporate specific religious values or practices, so that some days were dedicated to the divinities (called "unlucky days") or, on the contrary, dedicated to human public activity (called "lucky days").

Another important aspect of Roman religion was sacrifice. It was practiced on various occasions in order to ingratiate divinities, but despite various nuances between public and private rituals, the manner in which it was performed was always the same. Since sacrifice was intended as a sort of banquet served to gods, the offering consisted of animals, but also vegetables and liquids; the actual offeror of the sacrifice could even participate in the meal, which could not, however, be shared with Underworld divinities or Manes (shades of the departed) – in this case the offerings were completely burned. The most popular sacrificial victims were cattle and horses, considered a "superior" quality of sacrifice, with pigs and sheep considered "lesser" victims. Illustrations from various eras of Roman history (from the Republic to the end of the Empire) depict some aspects of these rituals (for instance, a *suovetaurilia* sacrifice can be seen on the altars of Domitius Ahenobarbus and of the *vicomagistri*, or on the Marcus Aurelius relief).

The fact that worship was always linked to a civic value, and not to faith, was a unique feature of Roman religion, confirmed by the fact that all rituals were closely linked to civic events.

54 - THIS MARBLE STATUE REFLECTS THE CAPITOLINE VENUS TYPE AND IS A COPY OF THE FAMOUS SCOPAS APHRODITE (350-330 BC) (CAPITOLINE MUSEUMS, ROME).

56 - THE CELEBRATED "FARNESE BULL" ENSEMBLE PORTRAYS THE TORMENT OF DIRCE TIED TO A BULL BY AMPHEON AND ZETHUS (NATIONAL ARCHAEOLOGICAL MUSEUM, NAPLES).

57 - ONE OF THE MOST IMPORTANT RITES IN ROMAN RELIGION WAS THE ONE CELEBRATED FOR THE FOUNDING OF A CITY. HERE IT IS SHOWN IN A FRESCO FROM THE ESQUILINE COLOMBARIUM.

58-59 - IN A COPY OF THE SCENE 98
OF TRAJAN'S COLUMN WE SEE, IN THE
BACKGROUND, THE SACRIFICE FOR
THE INAUGURATION OF A BRIDGE ACROSS
THE DANUBE (NATIONAL HISTORY
MUSEUM, BUCHAREST).

60 - THIS RELIEF SHOWS THE SACRIFICE WHICH
MARCUS AURELIUS CARRIED OUT AS *PONTIFEX
MAXIMUS* IN FRONT OF THE TEMPLE OF
JUPITER CAPITOLINUS ON THE CAMPIDOGLIO
(CAPITOLINE MUSEUMS, ROME).

60-61 - IN THIS RELIEF FROM TRAJAN'S
FORUM, WE SEE THE PREPARATIONS FOR A
SACRIFICE IN HONOR OF MARS WITH THE BULL
TO BE SACRIFICED AND THE TIBICEN TO PLAY
THE FLUTE MUSIC FOR THE RITUAL (THE
LOUVRE, PARIS).

Most Roman divinities had been assimilated directly through the Greek pantheon. Excluding the permanence of several original divine cults (Janus and Vesta, the latter nevertheless associated to the Greek goddess of the hearth, Hestía), the chief figure in the Roman pantheon was Jupiter, at the center of the Capitoline triad, alongside Juno and Minerva. The pantheon included the canonical divinities present in Greek religion, including Mercury (protector of commercial enterprise), Ceres (goddess of the harvest), Venus (love) and many others. They were flanked by personifications of aspects of daily life, like Time (*Aion*), *Fides*, and *Ops*. Contact with Alexandrian Hellenistic culture also spread worship of the figure of the emperor and his family, who were deified and often associated, even before death, to hero-demigod figures like Heracles (as in the famous example of the portrait of Commodus depicted with heroic attributes, like the *leonté* and a club). Emperors were deified after their death and this was then made public through monuments celebrating their apotheosis, as seen in one of antiquity's most famous reliefs, that of Antoninus Pius and his wife, the Empress Faustina. Successors of deceased emperors often dedicated to them temples and place of worship, which always retained a civic significance, a seal of political continuity with a specific imperial dynasty. Nevertheless, the cult of the de-

62 LEFT - THIS MARBLE STATUE FROM THE 1ST CENTURY AD SHOWS THE GODDESS MINERVA (TRIPOLI MUSEUM).

ified emperor never exceeded that of the chief divinities: it was simply a transfer of the devotion due to forebears in a family context to the extended Imperial sphere.

Roman religion was hallmarked by its civic and subsequently political connotations, but in times of crisis precisely these traits meant that it was flanked by other forms of religious expression, when private and more intimate aspects came to the fore and the public aspects were overshadowed. In the Imperial age this occurred with the diffusion of a number of oriental cults (for instance that of Mithras), then actually with Christianity itself, destined to become the state religion in AD 380, with an imperial edict issued by Theodosius.

Given the non-dogmatic and non-fideistic nature of official Roman religion, it was often subject to needs of State, or was simply returned to its cultural and intellectual sphere, as well as being flanked by many other private cults. When the "global" crisis of the 3rd century AD challenged all aspects of traditional Roman culture, as well as the empire's state, political and military organization, spiritual and religious matters tended to a privatistic and ethical form. This was the moment when the sun set on Roman religion, and simultaneously, with a series of collateral causes, the empire fell into decline and met its end.

62 CENTER - THIS ROMAN COIN FROM 235 BC SHOWS THE FIGURE OF JANUS IN RELIEF (BRITISH MUSEUM, LONDON).

62 RIGHT - THIS AURIC FROM THE NERO ERA REPRESENTS THE TEMPLE OF JANUS WITH ITS DOORS CLOSED AS A SIGN OF PEACE (CAPITOLINE MUSEUMS, ROME).

63 - THIS BUST FROM AD 190 PORTRAYS COMMODUS AS HERCULES, THE SEMIGOD THE EMPEROR IDENTIFIED WITH CONSIDER HIMSELF TO BE A GOD ON EARTH. THE SYMBOLS OF THE GOD: THE THUNDERBOLT AND THE CLUB, ARE CLEARLY VISIBLE.

64 - The supreme god in the Roman pantheon was Jupiter, portrayed in this statue in the classical style with a beard and wearing a leafy crown on his head, which is more visible in the head close-up. This type dates from the Greek original by the sculptor Briasside from the second half of the 4th century BC (National Archaeological Museum, Naples).

65 - This gigantic marble head portrays Juno (the "Ludovisi Juno") who, with Jupiter and Minerva comprised the "Capitoline triad". Juno wears a crown, a symbol of regality, decorated with palms (National Roman Museum, Rome).

66 - THE GOD APOLLO WAS ALSO INCLUDED IN THE ROMAN PANTHEON, AS IN THE GREEK ONE. SOME OF HIS ATTRIBUTES, SUCH AS THE LYRE PORTRAYED IN THE STATUE SHOWN, IDENTIFY HIM AS A PROTECTOR OF THE ARTS (TRIPOLI MUSEUM).

67 - A REFINED HAIR ARRANGEMENT WITH SHOULDER-LENGTH CURLS, FRAMES THE FACE OF THE GODDESS VENUS HERE PORTRAYED IN THIS 2ND CENTURY AD MARBLE STATUE WHICH REFLECTS THE CAPITOLINE VENUS MODEL (TRIPOLI MUSEUM).

68-69 - THIS BRONZE STATUE, FOUND IN POMPEII, PORTRAYS THE YOUNG GOD DIONYSUS OR THE NAKED BACCHUS, SEEN IN THE ACT OF RAISING HIS ARM AND POSSIBLY HOLDING GRAPES, WHICH ARE NOW LOST (POMPEII REPOSITORY).

70-71 - Other mythological figures were also associated with the cult of Dionysus; these include the Fauns, satyr-like beings with goat hooves. In the close-up of the hand we see a bunch of grapes symbolizing wine and feasts which were under the protection of the god Dionysus (Capitoline Museums, Rome).

72-73 - IN THIS FRESCO OF THE HOUSE OF THE VETTII IN POMPEII, ATTRIBUTED TO THE SO-CALLED 4TH STYLE, HERCULES, THE INFANT, IS STRANGLING THE TWO SERPENTS WHICH, ACCORDING TO MYTH, WERE SENT BY JUNO TO KILL THE CHILD BORN FROM THE UNION OF JUPITER AND ALCMENA. THIS SCENE TAKES PLACE UNDER THE WORRIED GAZE OF JUPITER, ALCMENA AND AMFITRYON, HER HUSBAND.

73 - THE MYTH OF THE CHILD HERCULES SLAYING THE SERPENTS IS PORTRAYED IN THIS MARBLE STATUE FROM 2ND CENTURY AD (CAPITOLINE MUSEUMS, ROME).

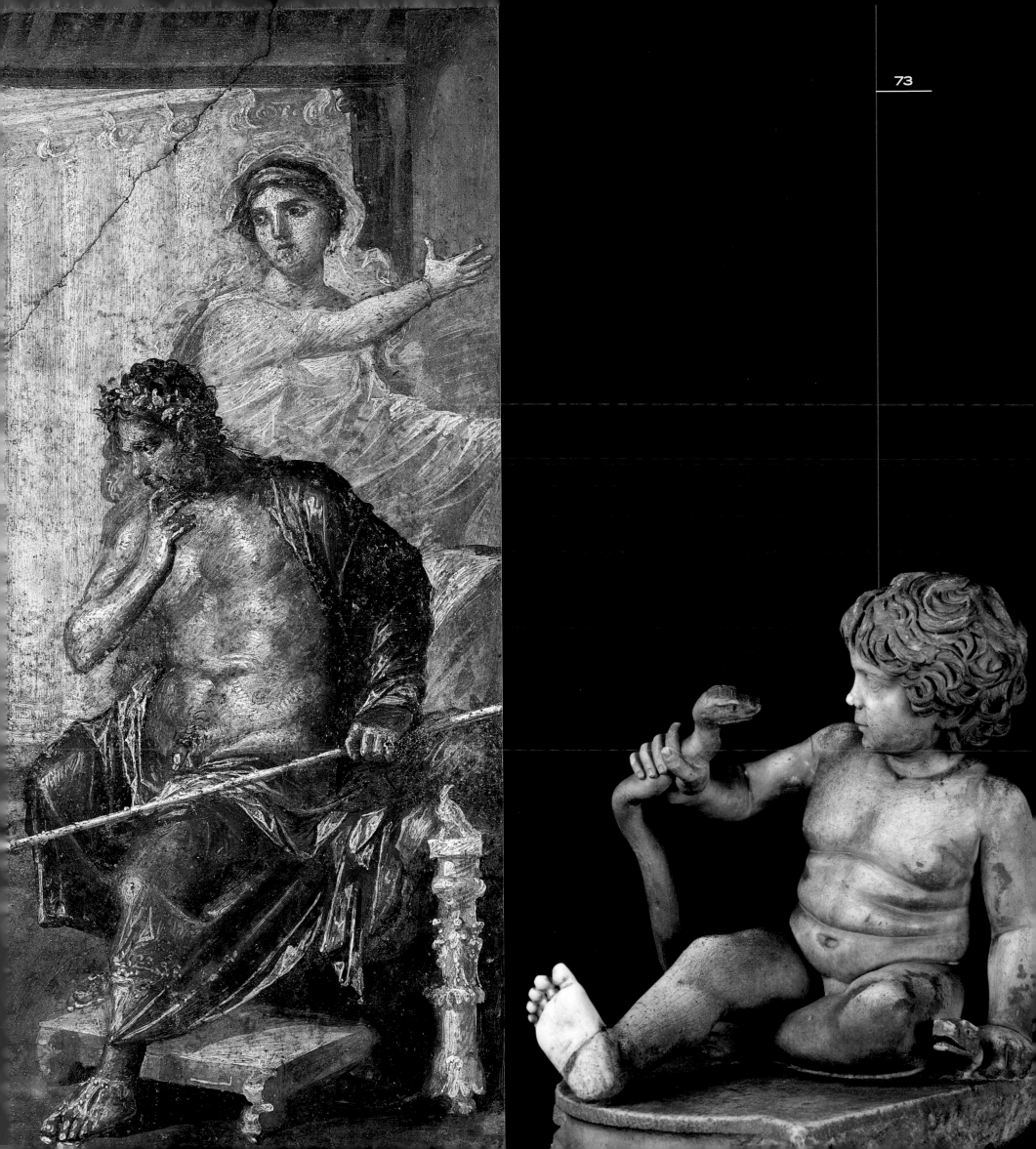

THE ARMY

Rome owed much of its fortune to human potential, which allowed it to train, maintain and develop an army that successfully left its mark on major historic events. In point of fact, the army can be considered not so much an apparatus of Rome's culture and power, but more a kingpin, so rooted in the State's cultural, political and economic dimension that it cannot be separated from the Roman civil context. The army also proved to be a potent tool for transmitting cultural and commercial models, to the point that all products of Roman civilization soon established themselves, through the army, across the entire territory controlled by Rome. One example is the widespread installation of the *castrum* as a layout model for newly founded colonies, or another instance is the adoption of typical Roman crockery (*terra sigillata*) by provincial populations, which arrived with the legions patrolling the *limes* (Imperial frontiers).

In the Monarchic era there was no professional army, simply a contingent of men at ease with weapons, who came from the three noble tribes (Ramnes, Tities, Luceres), and able to pay for their own arms. The group was commanded by two magistrates, one leading infantry and the other leading the cavalry (*tribunum militum* and *tribunum celerum*). The reform attributed to Servius Tullius brought differentiation, separating citizens who could provide heavy weaponry from those who could not. Moreover, a new combat system was introduced, with the use of hoplitic armor (Greek-style heavy armor for infantry) and Macedonian-type phalanxes (square formations). Despite the class division for the call to arms, with its implication of differing ranks and commands,

the lack of a real "professional" military, made it difficult to form a permanent army. Since most of the citizens called to arms were peasants, especially when enlistment was extended, they obviously had to neglect their work (and source of income) to serve the State. Later the hoplitic-phalanx system was abandoned, as battles were to be fought in rugged or impenetrable terrain, and was replaced by the manipular system that employed smaller units.

In basic terms, the army was based on the legion, where the infantry, by that time the core of the army, was split into three echelons: *hastati*, *principes* and *triarii*.

Depending on the type of armament used, the three groups were thus defined : *hastate* and *principes* carried the *pilum* (a weapon to be thrown like a javelin) and deployed the front line; the *triarii*, who made the final attack, were armed with long spears (*hasta*). The legionary infantry was organized in *centuriae*, led by a centurion, whereas the cavalry was grouped as *turmae* (30-man squadrons), and commanded by a decurion. Then, from the late 3rd century BC, a sort of light infantry, called the *velites*, went in to fight alongside the *hastati*.

Rome's ongoing expansion often called citizens to arms for periods lasting several years. This led not only to discontent, but also to widespread poverty among peasants and small landowners, who were the underpinning of the army but were unable to go about their business. In 107 BC, Marius, who also chose the eagle as the legionary icon, instituted a reform that was to revolutionize army structure: this was the start of voluntary enrolment, with no class requirements, and a concept that enabled the formation of a pro-

74 - In the close-up of the sarcophagus of a Roman general under Marcus Aurelius (AD 180-190) by Portonaccio, we see a battle scene with details of the armaments (National Roman Museum, Rome).

75 - In this relief, we see a battle scene between a barbarian, recognizable because of his long hair, and a Roman legionary, with plumed helmet and scaled armor (The Louvre, Paris).

76 - This relief decorates the breastplate of the armor of Henry II, king of France (1547-1559). This scene shows the Roman camp of Augustus who is being presented with the head of Mark Antony (The Louvre, Paris).

77 left - This small bronze statue portrays a legionary wearing typical segmented armor (British Museum, London).

77 right - This bronze Roman infantry helmet shows cheek and neck plates which are more evident than in the simpler "jockey-like" armor, and which were inspired by the Celtic helmet.

fessional army. For many, military service became a livelihood and often a real profession. This fact eventually reinforced the ties between soldiers and their general, who was therefore able to deploy this powerful army at his disposal, with all the consequent political implications. In fact, soldiers were given remuneration and gifts by their commander; in addition, plots of land were granted to veterans retiring from military service. The 1st century BC was also a time when the legions began to change tactics: the cohort was developed as a new tactical unit, and the light infantry (*velites*) was abolished. Allied troops were replaced by auxiliaries (*auxilia*), like the Numidian or Gallic cavalry, or the Cretan archers.

Augustus ordered another reorganization of armed forces, when Rome downscaled its expansion and became aware that it needed to defend its provincial territories. At this point the army became stable and finally professional, reorganized in a way that remained largely intact for at least three centuries. In particular, a military career proved advantageous for provincials who were offered Roman citizenship when they enrolled, which meant an assured step-up on the social ladder for their families. This triggered a process that

led to the army's progressive "provincialization," and replaced the "proletarianization" phenomenon, which had been so obvious in the Republican army. Augustus also established that the emperor was to be supreme military commander, reinforcing his own power and preventing any "uprisings" among rebellious generals. For this purpose, a personal guard for the Emperor was created, the *cohortes praetoriae*, the famous Praetorian Guard, stationed in Rome, but obliged to follow the emperor during military campaigns.

In the Flavian era (AD 69-98), this guard was extended to include a cavalry formation, the *equites singulares Augusti*, enrolled with the *auxilia*, which confirmed the elitist nature of this part of the army. So the importance of the auxiliary troops grew, and they were split into cavalry *alae* (wings) and infantry *cohortes*, recruited among the provincials, who had proved themselves to be most suitable for combating barbarian populations. So it was no coincidence that the provincial army ranks later provided the "adopted" emperors who rose to power from the second century AD onwards, and whose most famous example was the Hispanic general, Trajan.

78 LEFT - THE CENTURION, AN IMPORTANT RANK IN THE ROMAN ARMY, HAD ARMOR WHICH DIFFERED FROM THE OTHERS BECAUSE ITS *LORICA* (BREASTPLATE) WAS OFTEN DECORATED WITH APPLIQUÉS AND THE SWORD (*SPATHA*) WAS A LONG ONE (MUSEUM OF ROMAN CIVILIZATION, ROME).

78 CENTER - THE STATUE OF THIS LEGIONARY HIGHLIGHTS HIS SEGMENTED ARMOR, "JOCKEY-LIKE" HELMET, RECTANGULAR SHIELD AND SHORT SWORD OR *GLADIUM* (MUSEUM OF ROMAN CIVILIZATION, ROME).

78 RIGHT - THE TYPICAL ARMOR OF ARCHERS WAS COMPRISED OF A BOW AND IN THIS CASE IT HAD A DOUBLE CURVATURE AS CAN BE SEEN IN THIS STATUE (MUSEUM OF ROMAN CIVILIZATION, ROME).

79 - THE PRAETORIAN GUARD, THE EMPEROR'S BODY-GUARDS, WAS CREATED IN AD 2, DURING AUGUSTUS' RULE. THEY WERE CHARACTERIZED BY THEIR CRESTED GREEK-TYPE HELMETS AND OVAL SHIELDS, SIMILAR TO THOSE OF THE AUXILIARIES (MUSEUM OF ROMAN CIVILIZATION, ROME).

80-81 - THIS CLOSE-UP OF SCENE 32
OF TRAJAN'S COLUMN ILLUSTRATES THE
TECHNIQUE USED BY THE DACIANS
TO BREAK THROUGH WALLS USING
A BATTERING RAM IN AN ATTACK ON
A ROMAN FORTRESS.

81 - THE ROMAN *TESTUDO* (TORTOISE)
TECHNIQUE USED IN THE LAST BATTLE OF
THE THIRD CAMPAIGN OF THE 1ST DACIAN
WAR (AD 101-102) IS SHOWN IN SCENE
71 ON TRAJAN'S COLUMN.

82-83 - IN THE RAID BY THE DACIANS
AGAINST A FORTIFIED ROMAN CAMP, WE
RECOGNIZE THREE SARMATION HEAVY
CAVALRYMEN BY THEIR SCALED ARMOR
(TRAJAN'S COLUMN, SCENE 31).

As far as the navy was concerned, it was not until after the war with Carthage that Rome acquired its own fleet, but in any case this was not stable until the Augustan period. The military developed a singular method of combat that enabled them to board enemy vessels and to fight on board, using the *corvus*, kind of armored gangplank. In general, however, for the entire Republican period, the Romans relied on their allies for naval operations and, again, it was Augustus who also reformed this part of the army by creating three fleets. One was stationed at Forum Iulii (Cividale del Friuli, near Udine) , in the valley at the mouth of the River Natisone, abolished in AD 69), another was in Ravenna, and the third was in Misenum, in the Bay of Naples), with maritime policing tasks and functions. Later other fleets were added, in particular for defense, and support of land troops on the Danube and on the Rhine.

In the 3rd and 4th centuries AD, the army also declined, evident from the progressive "barbarization" of troops, in other words with increasing recourse to the enrolment of barbarian populations. The problems arising in the defense of the frontiers, progressively more unstable, meant that a maneuverable army was preferred, so it could be moved, as required, to the critical zone of the moment. The army comprised *limitanei*, delegated to garrison the frontiers, and by *comitatenses* and *palatini*, stationed in various imperial capitals. Constantine finally brought the reform that defined a career path only for soldiers, separating military and civilian offices and powers, which had been the privilege of the senatorial and equestrian orders, and had interwoven incessantly throughout Roman history.

84-85 - THIS RELIEF SHOWS A SHIP OF THE ROMAN FLEET WITH MILITARY UNITS ON ITS DECK (VATICAN MUSEUMS, ROME).

85 - THE BOARDING OF THE SHIP BY SOLDIERS HIGHLIGHTS THE ARCHITECTURE OF THE CITY (TRAJAN'S COLUMN, SCENE 33).

3

MAJOR EVENTS OF THE
GREAT MEDITERRANEAN EMPIRE

A period of bitter conflict, following the death of Cae- sar, marked the end of the Republic. The establishment of a 10-year, then lifelong, dictatorship, and above all the sup- port Caesar was given by the army and the *clientes* (mili- tary veterans who had been promised land, and the in- habitants of Cisalpine Gaul, who had obtained the right to citizenship), had aroused the Senate's antipathy. Opposi- tion to Caesar had increased especially because he had been offered the title of king, although he had insistently refused to accept, and which would have destabilized sen- atorial hegemony. The outcome of the conspiracy plotted against Caesar was another civil war, with a number of battling factions: the Senate, the Caesaricides, as well as one of his closest associates, Mark Antony, and Octavian, Caesar's great-nephew and adopted son.

After Mark Antony's defeat in Northern Italy, at the hands of Cicero, consul at that time, Octavian allied with his old rival Mark Antony to destroy Caesar's assassins, and then establish a second triumvirate that also includ- ed Lepidus. The Caesaricides were defeated at Philippi in 42 BC, and the three triumvirs shared out the territory: Lepidus was given Africa and the islands opposite Italy; Mark Antony took the East, and Octavian took Italy and the West. In 33 BC, when the triumvirate's mandate ex- pired, Octavian attempted to take all power: war was de- clared. Mark Antony was totally defeated in the sea battle of Actium (31 BC) and took refuge at the Egyptian court of his beloved Cleopatra. The end is well-known: both preferred suicide to seeing Octavian take Alexandria and annex Egypt.

87 - THE ARMORED STATUE OF AUGUSTUS AT PRIMA PORTA PORTRAYS THE FOUNDER OF THE EMPIRE IN HIS ROLES OF EMPEROR, SUPREME CHIEF OF THE ARMY AND PACIFIER (VATICAN MUSEUMS, ROME).

88 - CLEOPATRA, QUEEN OF EGYPT, IS PORTRAYED WITH A SOPHISTICATED HAIR ARRANGEMENT AND WEARING A HEAD-COVERING SHAPED LIKE A FALCON TO ACCENTUATE HER DIVINE ORIGINS (CAPITOLINE MUSEUMS, ROME).

89 - THE CAMEO IN RED CORNELIAN PORTRAYS MARK ANTONY, OCTAVIAN'S ANTAGONIST, IN AN IMAGE WHICH DATES BACK TO 40-30 BC, BEFORE HIS DEFEAT IN THE BATTLE OF ACTIUM (BRITISH MUSEUM, LONDON).

The Senate endowed the victorious Octavian with the title of *Augustus*, and he collected such a list of offices that the all reins of power were in his hands until his death in AD 14. Yet he violated none of the Republic's traditional principles. Augustus' *auctoritas* lay in his merging of personal power with traditional power, hence achieving the respect of the Senate and the Republican judiciary: he actually assumed *tribunicia potestas* (the power of the tribunate) and the *imperium proconsulare maius* (the power over the imperial provinces). He was the *princeps* and, as such, renewed the structure of the state to seek peace and harmony (the *Pax Augusta*). In the religious field Augustus revived old cults and initiated an intense period of political building and restoration; in the politico-military field, he reformed the army, creating a permanent body of professionals. He also reorganized the provinces, making them either senatorial or imperial; he gave them new administration and military order, creating new social dynamics through a middle class of functionaries and bureaucrats. Lastly, Augustus also resolved the dynastic issue by introducing the adoption criterion, which guaranteed survival of the imperial institution right to the end. His successors also offered the guarantee of personal power and followed that line, both in the Julio-Claudian dynasty (AD 14-68), and in the Flavian (AD 69-96). In particular, Tiberius (AD 14-37) (adopted by Augustus) and Claudius (AD 41-54) were guarantors of the political equilibrium established by the *Pax Augusta*.

90 - THE EMPEROR, AUGUSTUS, IN THIS STATUE ON VIA LABICANA, APPEARS "VELATO CAPITE" (WITH HIS TOGA PULLED OVER HIS HEAD) (NATIONAL ROMAN MUSEUM, ROME).

91 LEFT - THE SUCCESSOR OF AUGUSTUS AND HIS ADOPTED SON, TIBERIUS, IS HERE PORTRAYED IN A HEROIC POSE (NATIONAL ARCHAEOLOGICAL MUSEUM, MADRID).

91 RIGHT — CLAUDIUS IS PORTRAYED ACCORDING TO THE ICONOGRAPHIC TENETS WHICH SEE HIM AS JUPITER WHILE HIS TEMPORAL CROWN DENOTES CONTINUITY WITH AUGUSTINE POLITICS (TRIPOLI MUSEUM).

Caligula (AD 37-41), Nero (AD 54-68) and Domitian (AD 81-96), on the other hand, were more inspired by Eastern models, introducing principles of autocracy and theocracy, whereas Vespasian (AD 69-79) and Titus (AD 79-81) conducted themselves as administrators of state resources. In the meantime, Imperial territory spread well beyond the limits (the Rhine, the Danube and the Euphrates) indicated by Augustus, and proceeded to occupy all the territory of *Germania Superior*, Britain, and the Palestinian region in the East. After Domitian's violent end, his successor Nerva (AD 96-98) "officially" imposed adoption rather than the hereditary line as the principle for succession, thus sidestepping discontinuity if a dynasty died out. In fact, he actually adopted a brilliant Spanish soldier, Trajan, who continued expansionist policy toward new territories and his successor Hadrian consolidated some conquests. In fact it was Trajan (AD 98-117) who conquered Dacia (commemorated in the column bearing his name, erected in the Forum) and Arabia Petraea (modern-day Jordan). As emperor Hadrian ordered completion of the conquest of Britain and defined its boundaries when he ordered the building the famous wall that bears his name. Trajan, in particular, was not only an outstanding general, but also a great emperor, improving interventions in public works in the capital and inaugurating that season known as the "Humanist Empire."

92 - TRAJAN'S MILITARY ACTIVITIES ALONG THE RHAETIAN *LIMES* IS SCULPTED IN THE SPIRALING STORY ON TRAJAN'S COLUMN; IN A COPY, WE SEE SOLDIERS CONSTRUCTING FORTIFIED BUILDINGS (NATIONAL HISTORY MUSEUM, BUCHAREST).

92-93 - THE PERSONIFICATION OF THE RIVER GOD, DANUBE, ON A COPY OF THE LOWER SPIRALS OF TRAJAN'S COLUMN (AD 110-113), WATCHES THE IMPERIAL ARMY WITH A VIEW OF A DACIAN CITY IN THE BACKGROUND (NATIONAL HISTORY MUSEUM, BUCHAREST).

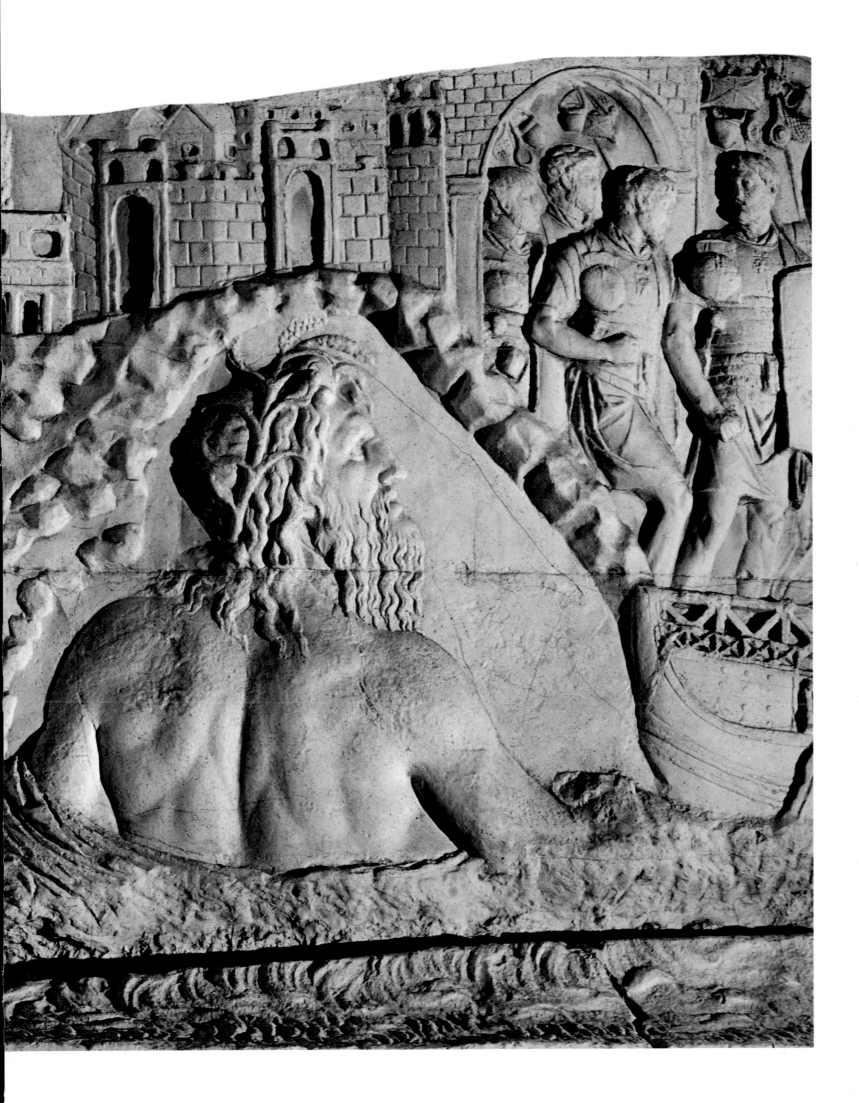

94-95 - THIS SCENE ON TRAJAN'S
COLUMN SHOWS A TYPICAL THEME IN
ROMAN TRIUMPHAL PAINTING: THE
DISCOURSE TO TROOPS BEFORE BATTLE.

95 - THE GREATEST OF THE EMPERORS
AFTER AUGUSTUS WAS TRAJAN, WHO
WAS ALSO FAMOUS FOR HIS MILITARY
CONQUESTS. HERE, HE IS PORTRAYED
ON AN IVORY PLAQUE WITH PART OF HIS
ARMY (2ND CENTURY AD) (EPHESUS
MUSEUM, SELCUK).

His policies were pursued by his successor Hadrian (AD 117-38) and the "philosopher" emperors, Antoninus Pius (AD 138-161) and Marcus Aurelius (AD 161-180), famous above all for their wise administration. When Marcus Aurelius died, he was succeeded (this time in direct lineage) by his son Commodus (AD 180-192), and the crisis that began to emerge continued throughout the 3rd century AD. There were many causes: the sheer cost of managing the military and internal politics, epidemics of plague, discontent and rebellion fueled by the army on the *limes* (the empire's military frontier in the center-north sector), provoking a profound emergency and ensuing civil war, following Commodus' assassination in AD 192. Once again, in these circumstances, victory fell to a governor (from Lower Pannonia, a territory corresponding more or less to what is now Hungary), Lucius Septimius Severus, from Leptis Magna (Labdah) in Tripolitania, supported by legions on the Danube and on the Rhine.

From AD 193 to 235, members of the Severan dynasty ruled in succession, definitively squashing the power of the great families who had formed the chain of power during the Republic, and Rome's predominance as the center of that power. Caracalla continued this trend of privileging the provinces as a political structure by extending Roman citizenship to all the empire's subjects.

96 - THIS RELIEF SHOWS THE EMPEROR, MARCUS AURELIUS, MAKING HIS TRIUMPHAL ENTRANCE ON A CHARIOT AFTER HAVING DEFEATED THE SARMATIANS AND THE GERMANS. THIS RELIEF IS PART OF AN ARCH ERECTED IN THE FORUM IN AD 176 (CAPITOLINE MUSEUMS, ROME).

97 - THIS PORTRAIT OF THE EMPEROR-PHILOSOPHER, MARCUS AURELIUS (AD 161-180) THROUGH THE REALISM OF ITS FACIAL FEATURES, SHOWS THE CHARACTERISTICS OF HIS REIGN WHICH AIMED TO GUARANTEE SAFE BORDERS (CAPITOLINE MUSEUMS, ROME).

The political building program commissioned by Septimius Severus also testifies to changes that tended to privilege and enhance the monumental appearance of his birthplace: Leptis Magna.

State organization imposed a rigid, authoritarian and centralized model, which was to culminate in Diocletian's reforms. Diocletian (AD 285-305) conceived a form of tetrarchy that actually endorsed the split between East and West, with separation of military and civil power. A concatenation of causes, including tax pressure for military needs, the *latifundia* crisis, the growing power of the provincial armies, monetary devaluation, combined with the spread of Christianity, all undermined the concept of the Roman State as the continuator of Alexander's empire and of Hellenism. This situation also affected the period's artistic expression and language, which became a manifestation of the malaise of the

time, but nevertheless detaching art from the canons of Hellenistic tradition. From a religious standpoint, Christianity (which Constantine's Edict of Milan in AD 313 officially sanctioned as the *religio licita* – the lawful religion) established itself as a focal point for life and ethics. Politically, transferring the capital to Constantinople, which became a new center of power for the early Constantinian dynasty, then the Valentinian and lastly the Theodosian dynasty, was to be the peremptory heralding of the decline of Rome's predominance, but also of the progressive crumbling of the Western Empire.

By AD 476, the progressive disintegration of the Western Empire, now in the hands of the barbarian populations, enabled Odoacer, a general of Germanic origins, to depose Romulus Augustulus, a child-emperor and last Roman ruler of the Western Empire, thus initiating the disintegration of the Mediterranean's political and religious unity.

98 LEFT - IN THIS COLOSSAL STATUE WE RECOGNIZE CONSTANTINE THE GREAT (CAPITOLINE MUSEUMS, ROME).

98 TOP RIGHT - IN THIS DIOCLETIAN AURIC (284-305), THE CREATOR OF THE TETRARCH SYSTEM IS CALLED P(IUS) F(ELIX) AUG(USTUS) (BRITISH MUSEUM, LONDON).

98 BOTTOM RIGHT - THIS SILVER COIN HAS AS ITS IMAGE THE EMPEROR CONSTANTINE THE GREAT (BRITISH MUSEUM, LONDON).

99 - CARACALLA IS PORTRAYED HERE FROWNING AND WITH HIS HEAD TURNED TO ONE SIDE (CAPITOLINE MUSEUMS, ROME).

ASPECTS OF IMPERIAL CITY-PLANNING IN ROME AND IN THE PROVINCES

From the early Imperial era, the image of Rome (*imago urbis*) as an archetypal city was established for urban planning, and was also applied to the towns in the empire's various provinces. Moreover, as soon as Rome's political and military dominion over a region had been recognized, the Romans sought to create new urban centers to replace the "old" capitals, whose image was bound to previous rulers. A typical and powerful example is that of the Celtic *oppidum* (town), Bibracte, a point of reference for the Aedui tribe, and where Vercingetorix, leader of the Gallic revolt against Caesar's occupation, finally surrendered. Following the definitive acquisition of Transalpine Gaul's territories and its transformation into a province, the Romans systematically deprived Bibracte of its role as a capital simply by establishing another town as the seat of Imperial power, just 15.5 miles (25 km) away. The new town of Augustusdunum (modern Autun), became the political and administrative center.

Rome applied the same system in other territories conquered in the West, replacing previously existing centers of power by new Roman ones. The towns in eastern provinces – like those in Greece or in Egypt – although they were distinguished by extensive historical and cultural underpinning, were also subjected to urban transformations, with the same objective of undermining the old regime with a new layout or-

dered by Roman authority. The urban fabric was imprinted with the significance of the sacred, and was cadenced by a sequence of altars (installed at crossroads) and temples, often dedicated to polyadic (civic) divinities, reaching as far as the heart of urban life, the Forum, with buildings set aside for political and administrative business. In synergy with this metropolitan "heart," there were also structures for commercial enterprise, such as the markets (*macella* and *tabernae*), and also the public baths, all built along the busiest main streets, obviously for the sake of convenience.

100 LEFT - A CHARACTERISTIC OF THE FOUNDING CITY WAS THE CONSTRUCTION OF CITY GATES AND THE PORTA PRAETORIA OF AOSTA IS AN EXAMPLE FROM THE AUGUSTAN ERA.

100 RIGHT - THE THEATER WAS ONE OF THE PUBLIC FACILITIES OF A ROMAN CITY; SHOWN HERE IS AN ARCH FROM THE THEATER AT AOSTA.

100-101 - THE VERONA ARENA IS ACTUALLY AN AMPHITHEATER AND AN EXAMPLE OF A GRANDIOSE MONUMENTAL STRUCTURE.

101 BOTTOM - THE HONORARY ARCH IS AN ARCHITECTURAL FEATURE OF THE ROMAN WORLD; HERE IS THE ONE IN AOSTA HONORING OCTAVIAN.

This almost mechanical imposition of an urban layout by Rome was offset by a minuscule exception, the spontaneous location of the theaters. Alongside the venues of political and business life, theaters were certainly preordained structures for a Roman town. In the Late Republican period, theaters were generally built in a central position – often linked to sacred sites like sanctuaries – in order to highlight their role for the amusement of the urban plebs, but equally to emphasize the significance and political scope in increasingly large social groups.

In colonies established in the Augustan era, however, theaters were built on the outskirts, and the most characteristic and famous is probably the theater of Augusta Praetoria (Aosta), built at a tangent to the city walls, near the Porta Praetoria (a major entry point). Similarly, the amphitheater, the other type of building designed for entertainment, was constructed in the suburbs, in keeping with an urban planning directive. Once again, there were political reasons behind this type of planning: when the Roman administration had established its rule and no longer required the support of the plebs, there was a tendency to isolate the space for entertaining this social stratum (theater and amphitheater) from the area set aside for the activities of municipal aristocracy, which was the forum.

The Imperial ideology that Augustus imposed was the underpinning of this sort of general urban planning that used urban models to imprint the mark of Rome across all conquered territories, not only in the Italian colonies but also in Gaul, Germany and Africa. Just a few of the "classic" examples of cities bearing this imprint are Verona, Leptis

Magna, Augusta Raurica (Basel) and Timgad (in Algeria).

It was not just the urban model that Rome diffused through the provinces. The same building techniques were also employed, especially *opus reticulatum* (concrete faced with slabs of tufa) and brickwork - although this was not completely developed at the time - which gave an immediate signal of the capital's presence.

As had already occurred for the colonies on Italian territory, a central model emerged in both the western and eastern provinces, serving as a monumental image for the towns. The series of buildings and areas that characterized town centers could be recognized in the civic-commercial district (the forum), with buildings earmarked for administrative purposes, and a temple as the center of religious life, with an area for amusement and entertainment, buildings for performances (the theater and amphitheater) and the public baths. Then there might be several commemorative monuments, including honorary arches, or other buildings with practical functions, like the *macella*.

The preferred model of forum in the West comprised a square with three sides closed off by arcades and the fourth side closed by a basilica, usually with a hexastyle temple, as can be seen in Nemausus (Nîmes), Lutetia (Paris), Alesia (Alise Ste-Reine), Lugdunum (Lyon) in Gaul, and also in Calleva

(Silchester) and Londinium (London) in Britain and in Augusta Raurica (Basel), etc.

On the other hand, the eastern provinces were distinguished by the so-called "arcade streets," a sort of covered monumental route, often with monumental access gates. Moreover, in the eastern towns it became popular to enhance entertainment buildings, like theaters, with monumental stage façades (for instance Ephesus, Miletus, Hierapolis, etc). In the African provinces, however, the most popular architectural genre imported from the capital was the honorary arch (for instance, Trajan's arch at Timgad, or that of Septimius Severus at Leptis Magna).

102 - THE ROMAN URBAN MODEL SPREAD TO THE PROVINCES, AND IN *GALLIA NARBONENSIS* THE MONUMENTS INCLUDE THE ARELATE AMPHITHEATER (ARLES).

102-103 - THE AQUEDUCT-BRIDGE (PONT-DU-GARD) OF NEMAUSUS (NÎMES), BUILT BY AGRIPPA, IS A FINE EXAMPLE OF STRUCTURAL SOLIDITY.

103 TOP - A FAMOUS EXAMPLE OF AN HONORARY ARCH IS IN ORANGE (ARAUSIUM) FROM THE TIBERIAN ERA (30-26 BC).

103 BOTTOM - THE TEMPLE IN VIENNE (FRANCE), DEDICATED TO ROME AND AUGUSTUS, IMPORTED THE ROMAN-ITALIC TEMPLE MODEL TO THE PROVINCES; ANOTHER EXAMPLE OF IMPORTED STYLE IS THE COEVAL MAISON CARRÉE IN NÎMES (AUGUSTAN ERA).

104 TOP - THE SERAPIDE BLOCK IN OSTIA ANTICA, FROM HADRIAN'S ERA, HAS AN INTERNAL COURTYARD WITH RECTANGULAR PILLARS.

104 CENTER - THE SQUARE OF CORPORATIONS IN OSTIA STILL MAINTAINS ITS BLACK AND WHITE MOSAICS WITH THE SYMBOLS OF THE CATEGORIES OF MERCHANTS (MARITIME) ASSIGNED TO THE COMMERCIAL AREAS.

104 BOTTOM - THE SO-CALLED TEMPLE OF CERES NEAR THE SQUARE OF CORPORATIONS; THE TEMPLE IS ON A HIGH PODIUM AND HAS A PRONAOS WITH TWO CORINTHIAN COLUMNS. IT WAS BUILT BETWEEN 90 AND 60 BC BY P. LUCILIUS GAMALA, BUT IS OF UNCERTAIN ATTRIBUTION.

104-105 - IN THIS BIRD'S-EYE VIEW OF OSTIA ANTICA, NEAR AN CURVE OF THE TIBER RIVER, A THEATER IS SEEN IN THE FOREFRONT BETWEEN THE SQUARE OF CORPORATIONS AND THE DECUMANUS MAXIMUS.

106-107 - In this bird's-eye view of the northwestern quarters of Pompeii, on the left-hand side we see the *macellum* building with a *tholos* or bee-hive structure for the fish market.

107 top left - The colonnade on the northern side of the Civic Forum of Pompeii impressively terminated in honorary arches in marble-covered brick; in the background we see one of the ruins.

107 top right - Via degli Augustali crossed Pompeii's Regio VII to connect the Forum area to Via Stabiana (cardus).

107 bottom - The amphitheater of Pompeii (70 BC), built by Statilius Taurus, is one of the most ancient examples of this type of architecture still standing. In the background, landscape Vesuvius is visible.

108 LEFT - THE GARDEN SURROUNDED BY THE CORINTHIAN PERISTYLE OF THE HOUSE OF THE VETTII WAS EMBELLISHED WITH MARBLE STATUES, HERMES BUSTS AND BASINS.

108-109 - THIS VIEW SHOWS THE *PRAEDIA* OF IULIA FELIX AND THE HOUSE OF VENUS FROM THE SEASHELL.

109 - THE HOUSE OF THE FAUN SHOWS ITS MAGNIFICENCE AT ITS ENTRANCE (*ATRIUM*) WITH AN *IMPLUVIUM* FOR RAINWATER DECORATED USING THE *OPUS SECTILE* TECHNIQUE; BELOW IS A VIEW OF THE PERISTYLE.

110-111 - THE WALLS OF THE
TABLINUM OF THE RESIDENCE
OF MARCUS LUCRETIUS
FRONTO IN POMPEII ARE
DECORATED IN THE III STYLE
WITH FAUX ARCHITECTURAL
DECORATIONS FRAMING
THE *PINACHES*.

111 TOP - THE *OECUS* OF THE
HOUSE OF THE VETTII
IS DECORATED WITH
EXTRAORDINARY PAINTINGS.

111 BOTTOM - THE *DOMUS* OF
PAQUIO PROCULO (CUPIO PANSA)
HAS A MAGNIFICENT MOSAIC.

112-113 - The domus of Gemma in Herculaneum was in the Thermae quarter; note the *atrium* in the foreground with its remaining wall decorations.

113 TOP - THE *TRICLINIUM* OF THE HOUSE OF NEPTUNE AND ANPHITRITE IN HERCULANEUM IS DECORATED WITH THIS PRECIOUS MOSAIC IN GLASS PASTE WHICH CAN BE SEEN AT ITS ENTRANCE AND WHICH GAVE THE RESIDENCE ITS NAME.

113 CENTER - AT THE INTERSECTION BETWEEN THE LOWER *DECUMANUS* AND THE *CARDUS* V, AN IMPORTANT HERCULANEUM INTERSECTION, WE SEE THE FOUNTAIN OF NEPTUNE.

113 BOTTOM - THE FOUNTAIN IN THE ATRIUM, WITH TWO SERIES OF OVERLAPPING ARCHES, OF THE SUBURBAN THERMAE OF HERCULANEUM WAS FILLED WITH WATER WHICH FLOWED FROM A BUST OF APOLLO PLACED OVER THE *LABRUM* (BASIN).

114-115 - The Merida theater (Augusta Emerita, founded in 25 BC) has a magnificent well-preserved frontispiece with some statues *in situ*; it was located outside of the city walls like the amphitheater and the circus.

115 top - The Temple of Diana in Merida has a classical architectonical layout with podium, Corinthian order and trabeation which curves in correspondence with the central intercolumns.

115 center - The amphitheater of Italica (Spain), birthplace of emperors Trajan and Hadrian, is one of the largest in the Roman world; enlarged in the Trajan-Hadrian period, measures 512 x 407 ft (156 x 124 m).

115 bottom - These two examples of polychrome mosaics from the 2nd century AD, which decorated Italica residences, show a strong Roman influence and were in fact completed in iconographic layouts which were popular throughout the Roman Empire.

116-117 - THE RUINS OF THE SEGOVIA AQUEDUCT (1ST CENTURY AD), WHICH CROSSED THROUGH THE CITY, SHOW A DOUBLE ROW OF ARCHWAYS IN GRANITE BLOCKS THAT ARE PRESERVED FOR 2388 FT (728 M), WITH A MAXIMUM HEIGHT OF 95 FT (29 M).

117 TOP AND BOTTOM LEFT - OF THE THREE AQUEDUCTS WHICH SERVED MERIDA, TWO ARE STILL STANDING: THE SAN LAZZARO (TOP) AND THE LOS MILAGROS (BOTTOM). SAN LAZZARO IS THE MORE ELEGANT BUT IS LESS WELL PRESERVED; LOS MILAGROS RISES 82 FT (25 M), HAS 37 REMAINING PYLONS IN ALTERNATING ROWS OF GRANITE AND BRICK, AND HAS THREE ROWS OF ARCHWAYS EXTENDING 2725 FT (830 M).

117 BOTTOM RIGHT - THE MERIDA BRIDGE ON THE GUADIANA RIVER, WITH ITS 60 ARCHES AND ITS LENGTH OF 2600 FT (792 M), IS THE LONGEST ONE IN THE ROMAN WORLD.

118 TOP - THE EPHESUS THEATER (TURKEY), INTO WHICH RAN THE VIA ARCADIANA, IS A HELLENISTIC CONSTRUCTION WHICH WAS LATER TRANSFORMED BY THE ROMANS. ITS MOST CHARACTERISTIC FEATURE IS ITS *CAVEA*, BUILT ACCORDING TO THE SLOPE OF THE TERRAIN.

118 CENTER LEFT - THIS DETAIL SHOWS THE CORRIDOR USED TO ACCESS THE LIBRARY OF CELSUS AND, IN PROFILE, THE ALLEGORICAL STATUES OF THE VIRTUES ATTRIBUTED TO HIM WHICH ARE IN THE NICHES BETWEEN THE ENTRANCE DOORS.

118 CENTER RIGHT - THE REMAINS OF ONE OF THE PILLARED STREETS OF EPHESUS, A TYPICAL STRUCTURE IN THE HELLENISTIC WORLD AND LATER WIDESPREAD IN THE CITIES IN THE EASTERN PROVINCES OF THE ROMAN EMPIRE, WITH THE RUINS OF THE PORTICOES ALONG ITS SIDES.

118 BOTTOM - THE TEMPLE DEDICATED TO HADRIAN IN EPHESUS HAS A RICHLY DECORATED STRUCTURE; THE DETAIL SHOWS THE TRABEATION WHICH CURVES IN AN ARCH IN CORRESPONDENCE WITH THE CENTRAL INTERCOLUMNS OF THE FAÇADE.

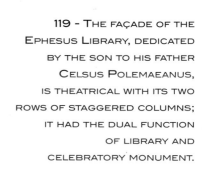

119 - THE FAÇADE OF THE EPHESUS LIBRARY, DEDICATED BY THE SON TO HIS FATHER CELSUS POLEMAEANUS, IS THEATRICAL WITH ITS TWO ROWS OF STAGGERED COLUMNS; IT HAD THE DUAL FUNCTION OF LIBRARY AND CELEBRATORY MONUMENT.

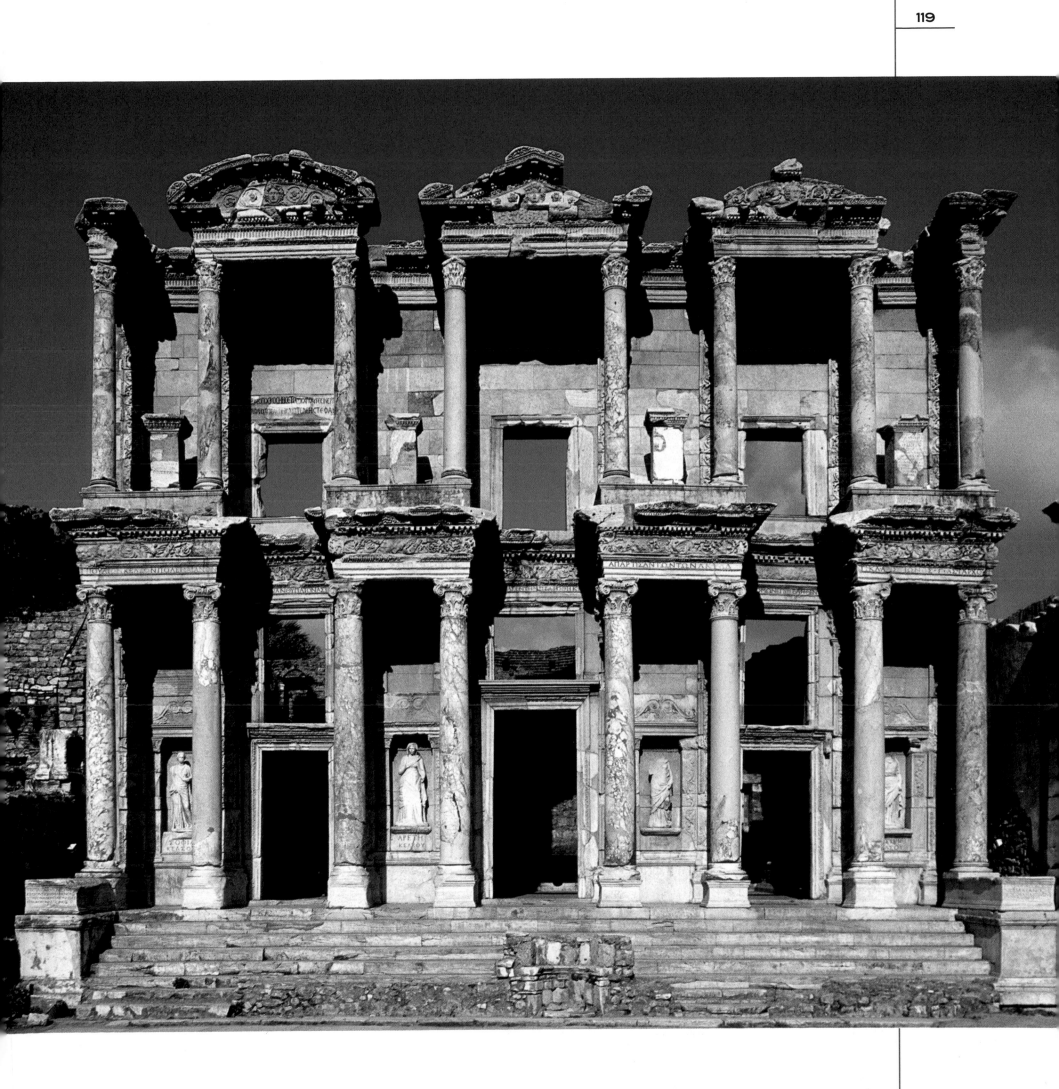

120-121 - THE TETRAPYLON OF APHRODISIAS PROVIDED A MONUMENTAL ENTRANCE TO THIS 2ND CENTURY AD CITY; ITS RAISED PLATFORM SHOWS ALTERNATING SMOOTH AND GROOVED COLUMNS TOPPED WITH FRONTONS DECORATED WITH VICTORIES AND CUPIDS SCULPTURE.

121 LEFT - THE THREE THEATERS OF APHRODISIAS, ASPENDOS AND MILETUS (TURKEY) EXEMPLIFY THREE IMPORTANT STYLES: THE APHRODISIAS ONE (30 BC) HAS THE FLAVIAN BASILICA IN ITS BACKGROUND, THE ASPENDOS ONE (AD 161-180), BY THE ARCHITECT ZENO OF THEODORE, IS AN EXAMPLE OF THE ASIAN-ROMAN ARCHITECTURE OF THE HELLENISTIC TRADITION AND THE MILETUS THEATER IS CHARACTERIZED BY THE SECOND *SCAENA* (STAGE) WITH THREE ROWS OF COLUMNS WHICH OPENED ONTO AN EXEDRA WITH A DIAPHRAGM OF COLUMNS.

121 TOP RIGHT - THIS MONUMENTAL ENTRANCE DOOR IS FLANKED BY TWO ROWS OF COLUMNS AND GAVE ACCESS TO THE THERMAE AND GYMNASIUM COMPLEX OF SARDIS, THE ANCIENT CAPITAL OF LYDIA. IT WAS BUILT DURING THE REIGN OF CARACALLA AND GETA (AD 211-217).

122-123 - THIS FUNERARY MONUMENT AS
CORINTHIAN HEXASTYLE TEMPLE OF
PALMYRA (SYRIA) SHOWS THE MONUMENTAL
LAYOUT OF THE CARAVAN CITY DURING ITS
PERIOD OF MAXIMUM SPLENDOR. OTHER
MONUMENTS ARE ALSO SEEN INCLUDING
THE REMAINS OF A COLONNADED VIA
AND, IN THE BACKGROUND, THE 13TH
CENTURY FORTRESS DATING BACK TO
THE TIME OF ARAB DOMINION.

123 TOP AND CENTER - THE TEMPLE OF BACCHUS AT BAALBEK (LEBANON), THE ANCIENT HELIOPOLIS, WAS ADORNED WITH WINDING ARCHITECTURAL DECORATION WITH GARLANDS OF GREENERY (TOP). THE NTERIOR OF THE CELLA (CENTER) SHOWS A WALL WITH A DOUBLE ROW OF SMALL ARCHES AND NICHES BETWEEN THE ROWS OF CORINTHIAN SEMICOLUMNS.

123 BOTTOM - ONE OF THE MOST SIGNIFICANT MONUMENTS OF PALMYRA IS THE SEVERAN HONORARY ARCH WITH THREE FORNICES (AD 220), WHICH FRAMES ONE OF THE COLONNADED ROADS.

124 TOP - THIS MALE TORSO IN MARBLE IS ONE OF THE MANY PIECES OF SCULPTURE FOUND IN CAESAREA MARITIMA (ISRAEL), CAPITAL OF THE PROVINCE OF JUDEA (AND LATER ALSO OF PALESTINE) FROM AD 44, FOUNDED *EX NOVO* BY HEROD THE GREAT AND KNOWN FOR ITS FAMOUS PORT OF SEBASTOS.

124 CENTER - THIS WAS ONE OF THE TWO AQUEDUCTS WHICH SERVED CAESAREA AND IT HAD A SINGLE ARCHWAY. IT WAS ALSO USED BY THE ARABS WHO TOOK THE CITY FROM ROMAN RULE.

124 BOTTOM - A MONUMENT IN CAESARIA WHICH TESTIFIES TO ROMAN INFLUENCE IS THE THEATER WHICH HAS BEEN COMPLETELY RECONSTRUCTED. THE DETAIL SHOWS PART OF THE *CAVEA*.

124-125 - THIS VIEW IS OF THE CITY OF BETH SHEAN (ISRAEL), THE SCYTOPOLIS OF THE PTOLEMIES, AT THE FOOT OF BEISAN HILL. THE ROMAN ERA LAYOUT CAN BE NOTED WITH A LARGE COLONNADED VIA ENDING IN A THEATER FROM THE SEVERAN ERA AND, ON ONE SIDE OF THE STREET, AN *ODEON*.

126 TOP - THE HERODION PALACE-MAUSOLEUM-FORTRESS (ISRAEL) WAS ONE OF THE HEROD'S NUMEROUS FORTRESSES. LINKED TO THE IMPERIAL CULT, IT HAD A CYLINDRICAL STRUCTURE WITH TOWERS AND A PALATIAL RESIDENCE AT ITS CENTER.

126 CENTER - THE FORTRESS OF MASADA (ISRAEL) STOOD ATOP A 984 FT (300 M) HIGH ROCK NEAR THE WESTERN SHORE OF THE RED SEA. ITS MAIN BUILDINGS, FROM HEROD'S ERA (37-4 BC), WERE: A PALACE, CASEMATES, AN ARSENAL AND LODGINGS

126 BOTTOM AND 126-127 - THE TWO VIEWS OF THE RECONSTRUCTED THEATER OF CAESAREA MARITIMA HIGHLIGHT THE VOLUMES OF THE CAVEA AND THE STRUCTURE OF THE PROSCENIUM.

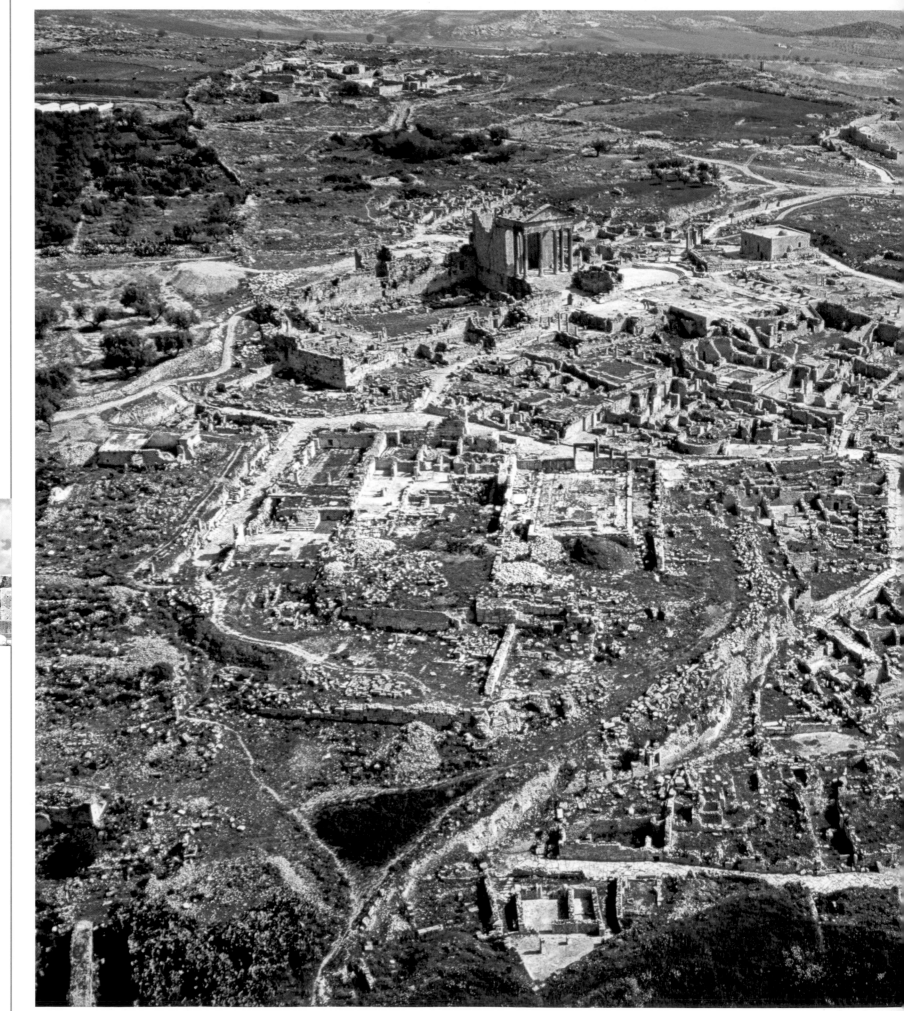

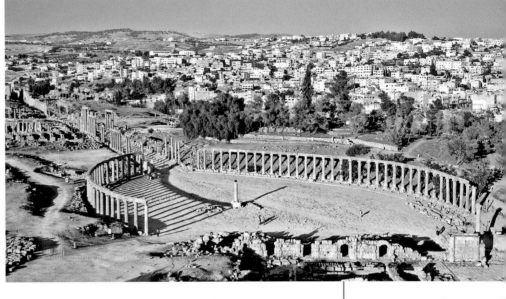

128 LEFT - THIS ARCHITECTURAL STRUCTURE FRAMES IN THE BACKGROUND THE *CAPITOLIUM* OF DOUGGA (TUNISIA), BUILT IN AD 166-167.

128-129 - THE CITY OF DOUGGA LIED ON THE SOUTHERN SLOPES OF A 1970 FT (600 M) HIGH HILL IN THE TUNISIAN TELL. IT WAS EMBELLISHED WITH MONUMENTS IN THE ANTONINE-SEVERAN ERA, ESPECIALLY THE FORUM WITH THE *CAPITOLIUM* AND SUMPTUOUS RESIDENCES WITH MOSAICS.

129 TOP - THE FORUM OF GERASA (JORDAN) IS CHARACTERIZED BY ITS UNIQUE OVAL SHAPE. A LARGE COLONNADED ROAD LED OUT FROM THIS AREA; IT SERVED AS THE CITY'S MAIN AXIS, ALONG WHICH ITS MAIN MONUMENTS WERE ALIGNED.

129 BOTTOM - THE THEATER OF BULLA REGIA (TUNISIA) HAS A WELL-PRESERVED STRUCTURE WHICH STILL SHOWS ITS CHARACTERISTIC BRICK WALLS.

130-131 - THE AMPHITHEATER, THE BUILDING FOR PUBLIC SPECTACLES CHARACTERISTIC OF THE ROMAN WORLD, IS WELL-REPRESENTED BY THE EXEMPLAR IN MAHDIA (TUNISIA) WITH ITS STILL INTACT ARENA.

131 TOP - THE AMPHITHEATER OF THYSDRUS (EL DJEM, TUNISIA) HAS AN ARCHED EXTERNAL STRUCTURE RESTING ON LARGE PILLARS, SIMILAR TO THE COLISEUM. THE CHROMATIC EFFECT WAS OBTAINED BY USING RED STONE FOR THE EXTERIOR AND POLYCHROME MARBLE FOR THE INTERIOR.

131 CENTER - THE BASILICA OF VOLUBILIS (MOROCCO) ON THE EASTERN SIDE OF THE FORUM SHOWS TWO APSES AND THREE ENTRANCES TOWARDS THE SQUARE. THE INTERIOR, INSTEAD, HAS THREE AISLES DECORATED WITH MONUMENTAL COLUMNS.

131 BOTTOM - THE MOSAIC DECORATING THE RESIDENCES OF VOLUBILIS SHOW THE BATH OF DIANA WITH TWO NYMPHS AS THEIR MYTHOLOGICAL SUBJECT. NOTE DIANA'S QUIVER HANGING ON A TREE BRANCH.

132 TOP - THE REMAINING PORTION OF THE TEMPLE OF ISIS IN SABRATHA (LIBYA) SHOWS, IN THE BACKGROUND, A PINNACLE-LIKE PUNIC FUNEREAL MONUMENT DATING FROM THE PRIMITIVE SETTLEMENT (2ND CENTURY BC)

132 BOTTOM - THE THEATER OF SABRATHA IS ONE OF THE MOST IMPORTANT ONES IN AFRICA. HERE, THE DETAILS OF THE EXTERIOR WALLS WITH ARCHES AND PILLARS IN TWO ROWS AND OF THE SCENE IN THE BACKGROUND SHOULD BE NOTED.

132-133 - THE *CAVEA* OF THE THEATER OF SABRATHA IS DIVIDED INTO THREE BALCONIES AND SIX WEDGES, WHILE THE SUMPTUOUS FRONTISPIECE WAS ON A PULPIT WITH ALTERNATING SEMI-CIRCULAR AND RECTANGULAR NICHES WITH DECORATIONS IN RELIEF (LATE 2ND - EARLY 3RD CENTURY AD).

134-135 - IN THIS BIRD'S-EYE VIEW OF LEPTIS MAGNA (LIBYA) WE SEE THE VAST ARCHAEOLOGICAL AREA IN THE FOREGROUND WHICH INCLUDES THE FORUM (ON THE LEFT) AND THE SEVERAN BASILICA (ON THE RIGHT). TOWARDS THE SEA, WE CAN STILL CLEARLY SEE THE ORTHOGONAL URBAN LAYOUT OF THE AFRICAN CITY.

135 TOP - GORGON-HEAD DECORATION EMBELLISHED THE MEDALLIONS IN THE TRIANGULAR AREAS BETWEEN THE ARCHES OF THE SEVERAN FORUM.

135 CENTER - THE INTERIOR OF THE SEVERAN BASILICA WAS VERY RICHLY DECORATED: THE COLUMNS IN CIPOLIN ARE SURMOUNTED BY WHITE MARBLE ROMAN-ASIAN CAPITALS SHOWING ACANTHUS LEAVES AND LOTUS FLOWERS.

135 BOTTOM - THE PARTIALLY
RECONSTRUCTED ARCHES
OF THE PORTICO OF THE SEVERAN
FORUM ARE RICHLY DECORATED WITH
MEDALLIONS DEPICTING HEADS OF
GORGONS. IN THE BACKGROUND,
THE WALLS OF THE BASILICA ARE VISIBLE.

136 TOP - THE ARCH OF SEPTIMUS SEVERUS WAS ERECTED AT THE CROSSING OF THE TWO MAIN ROADS OF LEPTIS MAGNA THE *CARDUS* AND THE *DECUMANUS*. FOR THIS REASON, IT HAS A SQUARE STRUCTURE WITH FOUR FORNICES.

136 CENTER LEFT - THE *MACELLUM*, THE MARKET OF LEPTUS MAGNA, WAS A LARGE COURTYARD WHICH HAD TWO CIRCULAR *THOLOI* INSIDE IT WITH AN EXTERIOR OCTAGONAL COLONNADE. ONLY THE PERIMETER COLONNADE OF THE SECOND ONE REMAINS.

136 CENTER RIGHT - THE ARCH OF TIBERIUS WAS ERECTED IN LEPTIS MAGNA (AD 35)

ALONG THE PAVED *CARDUS*, ACCORDING TO THE WISHES OF THE SUCCESSOR OF AUGUSTUS.

136 BOTTOM - THE REMAINS OF ONE OF THE CIRCULAR PAVILIONS (*THOLOI*) OF THE MARKET ARE OPPOSITE A SMALL HONORARY ARCH (IN THE FOREGROUND) WITH PILLARS DECORATED IN RELIEF PORTRAYING TWO SHIPS.

136-137 – THE THEATER OF LEPTIS MAGNA, FROM THE AUGUSTAN ERA, TAKES PARTIAL ADVANTAGE OF A SLOPE IN THE TERRAIN TO SUPPORT THE *CAVEA*. THE DETAIL SHOWS THE REMAINS OF THE TEMPLE OF CERES BUILT ON THE TOP OF THE *CAVEA*, IN THE CENTER, IN AD 35-36.

On the whole, the provincial towns were embellished by celebratory architecture that the emperors commissioned, and their building development simply followed Rome's urban-planning reference and model.

By the end of the 1st century BC, Rome reflected important city-planning transformations. Caesar had already started his monumentalization scheme for the Republican Forum with several major projects, like replacing the Basilica Sempronia with the more impressive Basilica Iulia. This building's central area was surrounded by a double row of arcades, and it is set on two floors, as was seen in the Hellenistic *stoai* model. A more radical project led to the elimination of the old Comitium and Curia buildings, but the real building novelty that Caesar ordered was the creation of a new forum, the Forum Iulium. He was able to achieve this by demolishing and expropriating previous monuments, aiming to create new spatial relationships based upon the theories of Vitruvius. The sensation of length given to the entire complex was elegantly closed by the tall podium supporting the temple of Venus Genetrix, and whose role was to celebrate the divine origins of the *gens Iulia*.

Caesar's Forum became the model for the layout of subsequent Imperial Fora, above all that of Augustus, built perpendicular to the first, also adopting its same ideological mission. The Forum of Augustus was conceived as an extension of the Republican building, and was constructed to the same blueprint as Caesar's, imitating the central position of the temple, in this case dedicated to Mars Ultor, avenger of the murder of Caesar. Therefore the temple's scope and function were to celebrate the victories of the new *princeps*, and his war trophies were actually installed in the sanctuary. The building's decorative sculptures, depicting the Victories and plaques simulating the shape of shields and arms, contributed to underscoring the temple's nature of military celebration. The forum space was a well-defined iconographic agenda, with statues installed in the porticoes and lateral exedras: on the left, the figure of Aeneas and representatives of the *gens Iulia*; on the right, Romulus and the Republic's *summi viri* (greatest men).

The theme chosen was intended to justify Augustus' political program, with the new Hellentistic-type dynasty of divine descent on one hand (hence Aeneas), and on the other the direct heir and continuator of the Republican regime (hence Romulus and the *viri summi*). An identical iconographic and ideological model was subsequently used in the other celebratory monument of Augustus' power: the *Ara Pacis Augustae*. In the Forum of Augustus a variety of multicolored materials were used, and the chromatic effect that was achieved underscored the various functions provided by the structures. For instance the boundary wall used peperino (dark-colored) marble and Gabi stone, whereas cipolin (a light-colored marble) and Carrara marble were used for the columns and capitals, with white marble used for column bases. The Corinthian capital was the favorite, ending in a basket of acanthus leaves. The "classic" element was also echoed in the reproduction of the famous Caryatid statues, found in the Erechtheum porch on the Athens Acropolis. So Augustus' Forum presented a "mixture" of motifs that paid homage to Greek art, but restyled them both technically and iconographically, intending to create a new genre that would be suitable for universal imposition of the *princeps*' figure and style.

138 - In this view of the Augustine Forum we see the high podium upon which arose the Temple of Mars Ultor, named for him to revenge the slaying of Caesar, after the victory of Philippi (42 BC).

138-139 - From the Augustine Forum, we see the Temple of Mars Ultor, built after the victory of Philippi (42 BC), with the ruins of the columns and two hemicycles formerly holding statues of the ancestors of Rome and of Aeneas.

140-141 AND 141 BOTTOM - THE INTERIOR OF THE PANTHEON, BUILT BY AGRIPPA AND RESTORED IN HADRIAN'S PERIOD (AD 138), WAS LATER USED AS A MAUSOLEUM BY THE ITALIAN SOVEREIGNS. THE MAJESTIC CUPOLA WAS MADE OF VARIOUS MATERIALS WHICH BECAME LIGHTER AS THE CUPOLA ASCENDED IN HEIGHT IN ORDER TO LESSEN THE WAEIGHT OF THE DOME. IN THIS BIRD'S-EYE VIEW WE SEE THE EXTERIOR WITH ITS CUPOLA AND OCULUS AND THE PEDIMENT.

141 TOP - THE FRONTON BELONGS TO THE *PORTICUS OCTAVIAE* WHICH WAS BUILT IN CAMPUS MARTIUS DURING THE AUGUSTAN PERIOD IN PLACE OF THE *PORTICUS METELLI* AND WAS USED AS AN EXHIBITION GALLERY.

Augustus' urban-planning philosophy envisaged division of the metropolitan area into 14 *regiones*, which replaced the traditional four sectors of the Kingdom and Republic. The new areas – officialized in 7 BC – comprised several districts (*vici*) and were organized in such a fashion as to improve public and administrative services. Each was district controlled by the authority of a *vicomagister*, appointed annually, but reporting directly to the emperor, and was consequently able to exercise political and social control.

The interventions Augustus made in the construction sector also affected the areas that had been involved in earlier schemes promoted by Pompey and Caesar, in particular at Campus Martius, and in part on the private land adjacent to the property of M. Vipsanius Agrippa. Formerly a lieutenant of the *princeps*, Agrippa – having married Julia, the emperor's daughter – was officially part of the reigning dynasty. His most famous creation was the Pantheon, the building dedicated to the dynastic cult, deliberately built on his own land (oddly enough Pompey had been the previous owner), so that State administration was not involved in a public operation – of clear dynastic inspiration and Hellenistic imprint – since it was, in actual fact, still bound to the Republican regime. Agrippa also built Rome's first public baths, initiated the construction of several other facilities including the aqueduct system, both restoring the existing structures like Aqua Marcia, Aqua Appia and Anio Vetus, and also building new ones (Aqua Virgo and Aqua Iulia).

Subsequently the southern side of Campus Martius was completed, with the addition of the Theater of Marcellus, dedicated to the imperial family's designated heir, who had died at a young age. The building was associated with (in the temple of Apollo Sosianus) worship of the patron divinity of Augustus' victory over Mark Antony and Cleopatra at Actium. The erection of the Portico of Octavia in place of the Portico of Metellus (again applying Greek models that included a portico demarcation with one or more temples at the center), made it possible to create an exhibition space for art collections brought from Greece. In point of fact, Lysippus' group of statues (depicting a troop of horsemen at the Battle of Granicus) was installed opposite the two temples dedicated to Iuppiter Stator and Iuno Regina.

141 CENTER - ON THE LEFT, WE SEE THE THEATER OF MARCELLUS, BUILT IN 13 BC AND MADE OF TRAVERTINE WITH THREE ROWS OF ARCHES (THE LAST ONE LOST); IN THE BACKGROUND, THREE COLUMNS FROM THE SOSIAN TEMPLE OF APOLLO (34 BC).

142-143 AND **143** RIGHT - THE MAUSOLEUM OF AUGUSTUS HAS A CIRCULAR MOUND-LIKE SEPULCHER TYPICAL OF THE HELLENISTIC TRADITION. IT WAS DESTINED FOR THE ENTOMBMENT OF MEMBERS OF THE *GENS IULIA* AND FOR THE VENERATION OF THE DYNASTY.

143 LEFT - THE ENTRANCE TO THE ENCLOSURE WHICH HAD CONTAINED THE *ARA PACIS AUGUSTAE* (13-9 BC) HAS A RELIEF FRIEZE WHICH CELEBRATED THE ORIGINS OF ROME AND OF THE *GENS IULIA*: TO THE RIGHT, THE SACRIFICE OF AENEAS TO THE *PENATES* AND TO THE LEFT, THE *LUPERCALIA*.

Two of the most famous monuments of Augustus' principate, and possibly of the entire Roman period, were also built in Campus Martius: the Mausoleum of Augustus and the *Ara Pacis Augustae*. Both were built after the occupation of Egypt, so were closely bound to the Hellenistic-type concept of sovereignty; that is, designed to celebrate the reigning dynasty. The round mausoleum – a monumental tomb to be used by the family of the *princeps* – was modeled on the prototype of the funeral shrine of Mausolus, King of Caria (whose tomb gave rise to the word mausoleum). The architecture of Augustus' tomb, on the other hand, was inspired by the tomb of Alexander the Great, which Augustus had seen, but was obviously a Roman structure, although not lacking in references to Hellenistic culture. When Augustus died, Tiberius installed bronze panels on either side of the monument's entrance, inscribed with the *Res Gestae Augustae*, a literary opus in which Augustus narrated the years of his reign.

The *Ara Pacis Augustae* symbolizes, in a nutshell, the *princeps'* ideological-political program, also expressing its formal intentions. The altar is surrounded by a richly decorated marble enclosure and the friezes that decorate the walls are metaphorical illustrations of the main principles of Augustan policies. The short sides include allegories of Rome, of

the goddess Tellus (Mother Earth), and the dynasty's legendary origins, whereas the long walls show the actual dynastic cortège, including all the members of the *gens Iulia*, depicted in hierarchical position. The use of friezes recovers and alludes to the famous Parthenon model. The accessory decoration includes acanthus volutes in the lower order of the outer walls (a motif borrowed from Pergamum's Hellenistic tradition), associated to the festoons and bucranes (decorative ox skulls) depicted on the inside friezes, a reference to the ancient Italic world's sacrificial traditions. Hence, the recovery of Classic-type motifs was established as a reaction to the "baroque" taste that had been dominant, for instance, in the great architectures of Late Republican sanctuaries. A characteristic detail of the *Ara Pacis* was its connection to other architectural elements that surrounded it, and its well-designed location. In actual fact, the square where it was originally built served as the quadrant for an enormous sundial, the biggest of its kind that had ever been designed at that time. The bronze reference numbers that indicated the times and the signs of the zodiac were attached to the paving, and at the center of the square there was a gnomon – the obelisk that can now be seen in Piazza del Campidoglio. The position of the monument had also been calculated astrologically, so that on Augustus' birthday (26 September) the shadow of the obelisk was projected directly over the center of the *Ara*. The full impact of this particular urban installation is now irremediably lost because the monument was moved, in 1938, to a distant area and reinstalled in an impractical showcase. Architect Richard Meier's new museum, built specifically to house the *Ara Pacis*, aims to pay symbolic homage to the context and significance of the monuments that surrounded it.

The historian Suetonius (69/70 BC-post AD 103), the chief literary source describing many of the structures erected during the Augustan period, deliberately quotes the emperor's famous words: "he said he had found a city of brick and left a city of marble" (*De viris illustribus: Augustus*, 28). In the *Res Gestae* that he himself wrote, Augustus boasted that he had ordered the restoration of 82 temples.

146 RIGHT - THE GROTTO OF THE VILLA
OF TIBERIUS IN SPERLONGA HAD
A COMPOSITE LAYOUT WITH A ROUND POOL
CONNECTED TO A RECTANGULAR TUB
SURROUNDED BY A HEMICYCLE GROTTO
AND TO ANOTHER NYMPHAEUM.

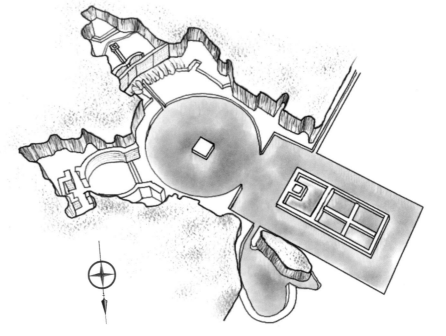

146 LEFT - THIS RECONSTRUCTION
SHOWS HOW VILLA IOVIS IN CAPRI,
BUILT BY THE EMPEROR TIBERIUS ON
A ROCKY PROMONTORY IN THE
NORTHEASTERN PART OF THE ISLAND,
WAS ORIGINALLY LOOKED.

The heirs of the Julio-Claudian dynasty – in particular Tiberius (AD 14-37) and Claudius (AD 41-54) – maintained Augustus' building policies, although not excessively interested in structures for prestige but nevertheless careful to restore existing works or to valorize the cult of the Emperor's deified figure. In fact, the *Ara Pietatis Augustae* was dedicated during the reign of Tiberius. This Emperor's building schemes are remembered mainly for what could be called the "extra-urban" structures: the *villae* he commissioned as a "buen retiro," perhaps in keeping with his solitary and melancholy character. So, apart from his famous villa on Capri, there was the Sperlonga villa on the Mediterranean coast, near Gaeta, remodeled over the existing Republican structure, near a grotto that seamlessly connected the landscape to the building, and acted as a scenographic backdrop where famous groups of statues were displayed. The latter narrated episodes from the *Odyssey* and were the work of Hellenistic sculptors of the Rhodes school (late 2nd century BC), for instance Agesandros, Athanadoros and Polydoros, probably also the authors of the Laocoön group. The groups of the blinding of Polyphemus, the assault of Scylla, the rape of Palladium, and Ulysses with the corpse of Achilles, have all been identified and reconstructed. It was Tiberius who began the construction of the imperial residence on the Palatine Hill, in Rome, near to what had been the home of Augustus. The objective of this building operation was to shake off the Republican image from the Roman dynasties, once and for all, but tended to increase their assimilation with the Hellenistic rulers.

The rule of Caligula was an exception in the framework of Julio-Claudian dynastic building programs. Despite the scant surviving traces of constructions in the urban-planning context, because of the *damnatio memoriae* ("damnation of memory," meaning "ondemnation to oblivion") that befell the emperor after his death, we do know that Caligula initiated an ambitious program of public works, possibly comparable to Nero's more programmatic and magniloquent scheme. Claudius, however, completed useful public works, especially aqueducts like the Aqua Claudia and Anio Novus, and was known for his connection with the "Republican" tradition, through application of a travertine block rustic ashlar, even on public monuments. The archetypal monument representing this trend is the so-called Porta Maggiore, actually a substruction of the Aqua Claudia aqueduct, which was an inversion of the Classical Augustan tendency, preferring a more Italic architectural expression, emerging specifically in the use of rustic ashlar.

Nevertheless, the "genius and excess" of Nero, perhaps unjustly criticized by the historiography of his own and even more recent times, is to be thanked for the most methodical urban plan of the Imperial age, although judged to be over-ambitious. The scheme was programmed and realized after the catastrophic fire of AD 64 (said to have been started by Nero himself) that destroyed many of Rome's *regiones*, with only 14 surviving intact. The urban plan envisaged a systematic and rational rebuilding of the destroyed districts, and it is another literary source, the historian Tacitus (AD 55-120?) – an eyewitness of the events – who illustrates the contents and defines the intentions of the scheme. Urban reform was intended in the modern sense and focused on regulations that controlled, for instance, the height of buildings, structural configuration, layout of quarters, etc. Therefore it was drawn up with attention to safety and hygiene, and emphasized fire prevention regulations in order to avoid any repetition of the previous disastrous incident. Consequently, the operation had more social than aesthetic content, and had been conceived in such a way as to prevent building speculation taking hold of the growing city, as well as making the metropolis more livable. At the same time, Nero was committed to installation of public services and new plants, for instance the public baths at Campus Martius. Later rebuilt by Severus Alexander (AD 222-235), this structure combined the Roman model with that of the Graeco-Hellenistic gymnasium, with a central hall and an axial symmetrical layout. This design was used for the Baths of Titus, in turn constructed in line with the *Domus Aurea* (the Golden House), and therefore felt by many to be the real baths area for Nero's residence. The construction program that Nero implemented also embraced other areas of the empire, for instance initiating works to create the Isthmus of Corinth, a connection between Misenum and Lake Avernus in the Bay of Naples area, or the canal system for connecting Ostia to Rome.

In AD 64 construction of the Emperor's residence, the *Domus Aurea*, was begun; it built on land acquired by demolishing, expropriating and confiscating buildings, and the new structure was partially erected over the remains of the previous *Domus Transitoria*. Nero's new residence was designed by the architects Severus and Celer, and comprised two components, the building and the landscape, perfectly integrated by a sequence of pavilions, gardens, coppices, fields and *vivaria* (special tanks for breeding fish). The latter revolved around a central nucleus called the *stagnum*, an artificial lake that was then dried out by the Flavian dynasty to make room for the Flavian amphitheater, better known as the Coliseum. The actual *Domus Aurea* then consisted

of a west wing, designed with peristyles (courtyards with porches), and an eastern wing, whose most unique element was the Octagonal Room, an area with a vaulted ceiling that was intended for formal reception purposes. In the *Domus Aurea* the architectural and pictorial elements blended perfectly: the latter were the work (or design) of the artist Fabullus, who decorated the walls and the ceilings in the *Domus* applying the Fourth Pompeian "fantastic and baroque" style. The entire construction expressed a deep interaction with the building tendencies of Roman architecture and Eastern Hellenistic models, applying a blueprint that clearly distinguished between areas for public encounters and those for personal use. This was a choice that reflected Nero's political dualism, since the emperor refused to associate his personality in the public works he built, but wanted acute personalization of his "living space." Suetonius states that the emperor actually said of the *Domus Aurea*: "At last I am able to live in a home worthy of a human being" (*De vita Caesarum: Nero*, 31), thereby underscoring the private nature of the building, which was not built in accordance with the canons applicable to the residence of the ruler of the empire.

147 - In this bird's-eye view we see the private residence of the emperor Nero, the *Domus Aurea* (AD 64-68). It was far more extensive than this partly excavated portion on the Oppian Hill.

As far as Nero was concerned, the *damnatio memoriae* reflected the policies of his successors, the Flavian dynasty, who concentrated on restoring to the public and private spaces that had been occupied by the emperor, which was a return to the programs of the Caesar-Augustans.

In point of fact, Rome's increasing population was creating space issues, which were a result by ignoring Nero's regulations limiting building height, but at the same time — demagogically — extending public areas in the monumental city center.

The *Forum Pacis*, whose very name echoes the *Pax Augusta* on one hand, and the triumph in the Jewish Wars on the other, was erected by Vespasian, south of the Roman Forum, by recovering an area that Nero had taken from the people. The square structure is reminiscent of the layout of a *castrum* (a military camp), but enhanced with porticoes and libraries, with the *Templum Pacis* placed centrally, at the back, and without a podium.

The anti-Nero operation was also completed by a sort of culture-museum recovery of most of the Greek works of art that the Emperor had removed from public display and installed in the *Domus Aurea*.

The most significant recovery, however, was that involving the space that had been occupied by Nero's private dwelling, one wing of which was partially inhabited by Titus. The baths named after the Emperor, as already mentioned, were merely "recovering" the baths area belonging to the *Domus*. On the other hand, the central area occupied by the

148 - THIS FRESCO IN A POMPEII HOME SHOWS A BRAWL IN THE AMPHITHEATER BETWEEN RESIDENTS OF POMPEII AND THOSE OF NOCERA (NATIONAL ARCHAEOLOGICAL MUSEUM, NAPLES).

148-149 AND 149 BOTTOM - THE COLISEUM, INAUGURATED BY TITUS IN AD 80, WAS BUILT OF TRAVERTINE WITH THREE ROWS OF ARCHES FRAMED BY COLUMNS AND THE LAST ROW WITH A CONTINUOUS WALL. BELOW, WE SEE THE UNDERGROUND STRUCTURES.

stagnum, once filled in, was given over to the construction of the great Flavian Amphitheater, better known as the Coliseum, the latter name due to a colossal statue of Nero, which was then modified and dedicated to Helios, the sun god.

The Coliseum is the first construction of this type completed in Rome using durable material, and it is as specifically significant because of the central position it occupies in the urban context, as well as for its sheer size and height, on an elliptical foundation.

150 AND 151 BOTTOM LEFT - THESE
THREE SMALL STATUES SHOW
GLADIATORS DRESSED FOR ATTACK WITH
VARIOUS TYPES OF WEAPONS, SHIELDS
AND HELMETS. THE TWO ON THE LEFT
ARE FROM POMPEII AND TESTIFY TO
POMPEII'S PASSION FOR THIS TYPE OF
SPECTACLE; THE ONE ON THE RIGHT,
INSTEAD, IS FROM THE AFRICAN
PROVINCES (NATIONAL
ARCHAEOLOGICAL
MUSEUM, NAPLES AND
SABRATHA MUSEUM).

150-151 - THIS CELEBRATED RELIEF
SHOWS A FOUR-HORSE CHARIOT RACE IN
ROME'S CIRCUS MAXIMUS
(ARCHAEOLOGICAL MUSEUM, FOLIGNO).

151 BOTTOM RIGHT - ONE OF THE TRIALS
THE GLADIATORS HAD TO FACE WAS TO
FIGHT SAVAGE BEASTS AS SEEN IN
THIS TERRACOTTA RELIEF (NATIONAL
ARCHAEOLOGICAL MUSEUM, AQUILEIA).

During Domitian's reign (AD 81-96), construction activities increased, in part because in AD 80 yet another fire had devastated the city. The Capitoline Hill and Campus Martius were almost completely restructured, and in the central area of the latter the Forum Transitorium was constructed, thus named as it was a thoroughfare from the Roman Forum to the Imperial Fora. The project was begun by Domitian but completed, in AD 97, by Nerva; thus it is known as the Forum of Nerva. It was a space dominated by a temple on a podium, in a central position, and dedicated to Minerva, but its perimeter had to be adapted to the boundaries imposed by the neighboring fora of Caesar and of Augustus, in particular to the exedra to the left of the Augustan complex. The most monumental opus built during Domitian's rule was undoubtedly the palace complex on the Palatine Hill. In this case the name of the architect who supervised the

Circus Maximus, a structure given over to entertainment and the presence of the plebs. The palace was built in brick and mix. From its inauguration Domitian's palace became the only official seat for Roman rulers, who never again built to diversify dwellings, and always established themselves in buildings concentrated in a single space, symbolic of the unitary quality of their power. Other works built during Domitian's reign include another stadium (lost to history, but which occupied the space now called Piazza Navona), and an arch erected in honor of his brother, Titus, in an eminent and significant position, at the end of the Roman Forum's Via Sacra.

Building activities in the capital peaked during the reign of Trajan (AD 98-117). A "provincial" emperor, born in Spain and adopted by Nerva, Trajan inaugurated a series of impressive works that were the result of cooperation with one of the most

project had been handed down through history: Rabirius, who appears twice in the *Epigrams* of the poet Martial (AD 40-104). The location was chosen for two types of reasons: the desire to render the complex independent of the city, and the functional aspect of seeking a defensive structure closer to the new vision of the sovereign's power. It was an outright imperial palace that distinguished itself from previous princely residences, not only from the "bourgeois" home of Augustus, but also from Nero's luxurious yet private *Domus Aurea*, since it was a unitary complex including public reception areas and residential areas, peristyles, gardens and a stadium. The main entrance of the *Domus Flavia* or *Augustana* opened on to the Forum, the exemplary site of political power, whereas the other side looked out over the

talented architects of the ancient world: Apollodorus of Damascus. It could be said that he was the first professional architect and he was also the author of a treatise on poliorcetics (siegecraft), which he wrote after his experience as a military architect in Trajan's retinue after the campaign against the Dacians. The most precise information regarding this military campaign can be found in the description sculpted on the Trajan Column, where Apollodorus is often depicted at the emperor's side, proving the close bond of collaboration between the two men. Moreover, the column also shows admirable illustrations of the works that were the fruit of Apollodorus' genius, including a bridge over the Danube (opposite the town of Drobeta), fortifications and military camps.

154 - THE DOMUS AUGUSTANA OF THE FLAVI PALACE ON THE PALATINE HILL WAS THE PRIVATE RESIDENCE OF EMPERORS AND IT LOOKED ONTO THE CIRCUS MAXIMUS THROUGH A TWO-LEVEL COLONNADED EXEDRA.

155 - IN THIS AERIAL VIEW OF THE PALATINE HILL, WE SEE THE *DOMUS FLAVIA* (ON THE LEFT) CONNECTED TO THE *DOMUS AUGUSTANA* (ON THE RIGHT) WITH THE IMPERIAL FORA IN THE BACKGROUND.

In the civil field, his greatest and most significant construction was precisely that resulting from his cooperation with the Emperor: the Forum of Trajan (also called the Forum Ulpium), the greatest in a group of Imperial Fora. The complex mimicked the layout of the *praetorium*, with a great central squared piazza, and was connected to the structure of Trajan's Marketplaces, which bestowed on the monument a dimension of daily life.

Trajan's Forum was an architectural masterpiece, built to eliminate the saddle that connected the Quirinal Hill with the Capitoline Hill, but which ended up by connecting the city's two greatest monumental complexes (the fora and Campus Martius). The complex, comprising a piazza and colonnade, with a statue of the emperor on horseback in the center, was closed on the short side by the Basilica Ulpia, with concentric aisles, set in a horizontal position. The basilica imitated the piazza's layout of two side apses and was itself closed off at the bottom by the *bibliothecae*, the Greek and the Latin libraries, separated in the center by the extremely famous marble column with spiral decoration narrating the Dacian War, and whose base was intended to store the Emperor's ashes.

The Forum was closed by an apsidated area, onto which opened the *templum divi Traiani* (temple of the Deified Trajan), which probably belonged to the subsequent period, that of Hadrian. The square's north-western hemicycle housed Trajan's Marketplaces, erected in the space between the Quirinal and the Subura, their brickwork and mix structure contrasting with the multicolored marble used for the Forum complex. The brick stamps (the factory branding imprinted on the bricks used to make the buildings) have made it possible to discover that the Markets were begun before the Forum, proof that it was a unitary project, defined as "secular" precisely because of the lack of a temple in the central position.

Even the relationship with the war narration by images on Trajan's Column underscores the intention of moving away from the monumentalization of the legends and history of the previous emperors. The Marketplaces' layout is split into two floors, one cadenced by a hemicycle and the other by the *tabernae* set on a split level, separated by Via Biberatica. Architecturally the complex is a perfect combination of Greek tendency and Roman elements, neither dominating the other, as is also documented by another great "civic" installation designed by Apollodorus: the Baths

of Trajan. This building filled the final piece of land left free by the *Domus Aurea*, covering a surface of about 118,500 sq. ft (11,000 sq. m). The symmetrical axial floorplan had been designed to lie in a precise direction, which governed the position of the *calidarium* and the *tepidarium* (rooms for hot and warm water baths), and this ensured they were always heated. The actual heart of the baths was right at the center of a fenced portico area, within which a garden had been included, with exedras and rooms that faced out onto the great central hemicycle on the longest side. The most obvious innovations compared to the layout of previous

Trajan's successor Hadrian (AD 117-138) initiated intense building activity in Rome. Apart from rebuilding Agrippa's Pantheon, destroyed by fire in AD 80 and constructed in the version still visible today, the emperor also commissioned another monumental building, a unique temple dedicated to Venus and Rome. The interior of this sanctuary, a pseudodipteral decastyle (i.e., with 10 columns on the short sides and 20 on the long sides), included a dual structure with two tangent cellas at the apse. The construction philosophy that Hadrian applied to the capital, as far as can be seen, intended to adopt the monumentalization of temples and to recover Asian canons. In this perspective the emperor dismissed Apollodorus, who disagreed with the new ruler's architectural concepts. Moreover, given developments in techniques for producing and using bricks, it was decided to rebuild entire districts in the capital's urban context, with multi-story *insulae*, in a scheme that extended as far as Ostia.

156-157 - IN THIS AERIAL PHOTO WE SEE ALL THE STRUCTURES OF TRAJAN'S FORUM: THE SQUARE CLOSED TRANSVERSELY BY THE BASILICA WITH THE COCLIDE COLUMN IN THE BACKGROUND AND, ON THE RIGHT, THE GREAT HEMICYCLE OF TRAJAN'S MARKETS WITH VIA BIBERATICA.

157 TOP - SCENE 5 OF TRAJAN'S COLUMN SHOWS THE ROMANS CROSSING A RIVER IN BOATS AND THE TROOPS MARCHING TO AN ENCAMPMENT.

157 BOTTOM - ON THIS SPIRAL OF TRAJAN'S COLUMN, WE SEE THE DEPARTURE OF THE TROOPS FOR THE FIRST DACIAN CAMPAIGN WITH TRAJAN, IN SCENE 10, ADDRESSING HIS TROOPS.

baths, however, were mainly the combined room functions, which were no longer simple spaces for personal hygiene, but now venues for meeting, culture and exercises, thereby combining in a pure Roman context the concept of the Greek gymnasia. The Baths of Trajan became a prototype for subsequent Imperial baths, as can be seen in later examples like the Baths of Caracalla and the Baths of Diocletian. Other public works worthy of mention from the Trajan period include the hexagonal port near Fiumicino, which was intended to extend the port installed by Claudius, and the triumphal arches at Ancona and Benevento.

However, the building project for which Hadrian is best remembered (also because it inspired Marguerite Yourcenar's novel *Memoirs of Hadrian*) must be a great palace-estate complex at Tivoli, also known as "Villa Adriana." The villa is closely bound to the emperor's personality and is almost a museum dedicated to his travels. It was here that he ordered true copies of the works of art that had impressed him, or paying homage in the structures to those monuments he had visited in the empire's territories. Each corner of the villa was hallmarked by some symbolic significance, culminating in a dedication to the heartbreaking memories of his beloved Antinous, extensively celebrated with statues that depict him in classical poses. Then there was the Canopus, an enormous artificial lake flanked by columns and statues, commemorating the emperor's trip to Egypt, not to mention the replica of the Erechtheum's Caryatids, which were the emblem of the city of Athens. The villa's complex structure is organized as a pavilion layout, and is strongly influenced by the "baroque" ele-

ment of Pergamene Hellenism, whose fulcrum was the circular maritime theater, around which other groups of buildings were installed. The estate and villa at Tivoli reinstated the philosophy of an emperor's private residence, which combined to the need for privacy and for concentration, with the desire to extend an area for personal feelings. In the city of Rome, Hadrian's urban planning envisaged another monumental building: a mausoleum for his own burial. This monument was subsumed in the Middle Ages by the Castel Sant'Angelo fortress, but its original circular layout resounded with Hellenistic precedents and resembled the mausoleum that Augustus had commissioned earlier.

158-159 - IN THIS VIEW OF HADRIAN'S VILLA (AD 130-138) WE SEE THE ENSEMBLE'S MAIN STRUCTURES: THE PECILE AND THE STADIUM (TOP LEFT), THE GREAT AND SMALL THERMAE (BELOW) AND (TOP RIGHT) THE MARITIME THEATER, THE STATION OF THE GUARDS AND THE HALL OF THE DORIC PILLARS.

159 - THESE STATUES WHICH REPRODUCE THE CARYATIDS OF THE ERECHTHEUM IN ATHENS ARE SOME OF THE COPIES OF GREEK ART WHICH DECORATED THE CANOPUS OF HADRIAN'S VILLA.

158 TOP - THE CANOPUS, THE NYMPHAEUM-TRICLINIUM OF HADRIAN'S VILLA, WAS A LONG BASIN OF WATER ENDING IN A PAVILION AND FRAMED BY A COLONNADE WITH NUMEROUS COPIES OF GREEK STATUES.

158 BOTTOM - A STRUCTURE ORIGINAL TO HADRIAN'S VILLA WAS THE "MARITIME THEATER", A SORT OF NYMPHAEUM-APARTMENT ENCLOSED IN A ROUND AREA AND SEPARATED BY A RING-SHAPED BASIN.

160-161 AND 161 - HADRIAN'S
MAUSOLEUM, INSPIRED BY MAUSOLEUM
OF AUGUSTUS, IS ON THE RIGHT SIDE OF
THE TIBER IN FRONT OF THE CAMPUS
MARTIUS AND IS CONNECTED TO IT BY
THE ELIO BRIDGE. IT'S A DRUM-LIKE
CONSTRUCTION ON A WHITE MARBLE
BASE WITH A MOUND SURMOUNTED BY
MONOPTEROS TOPPED WITH A BRONZE
STATUE OF THE EMPEROR ON A CHARIOT
(QUADRIGA). IT WAS TRANSFORMED INTO
A FORTRESS IN THE 5TH CENTURY AD
AND EXPANDED TO INCLUDE OTHER
STRUCTURES. TODAY, IT IS KNOWN AS
CASTEL SANT'ANGELO.

During his reign, Commodus (AD 177-192) initiated other urban reconstruction following yet another fire in AD 191, and which involved the Temple of Peace and the Portico of Octavia. The most impressive construction in the subsequent period, dominated by the Severan dynasty, was certainly the majestic façade added to the Imperial palace on the Palatine Hill, the so-called Septizodium. The Arch of Septimius Severus was built during the same period, in a key location, the north-west corner of the Roman Forum, fostering the monument's propagandistic effect: in fact, the arch was intended to celebrate the emperor's victorious campaigns in the East, against the Parthians. As far as the provinces were concerned, Septimius Severus implemented some significant building work in Leptis Magna, the town where he was born. He enhanced this African town with a series of monuments, including a great square-fronted arch that celebrated his victories over the Parthians. The combined allegorical-style illustration on the monument to the Imperial family (the emperor's wife, Julia Domna, is shown as a winged Victory) proves the historic importance given to the event. The town was also embellished in line with scenographic Hellenistic canons of architecture: a colonnaded street and a new Forum were built, and even private buildings included lavish villas with multicolored mosaics.

On the other hand, as far as Rome was concerned, the Baths of Caracalla were the last great public buildings to be erected, completed by the Septimius Severus' successors and which can be said to represent the peak of the city's evolution. The economic, social and military crises that overwhelmed the empire during the 3rd century AD also meant that building development stopped, enjoying a brief reprise at the time of Diocletian and the tetrarchy. The disastrous fire that enveloped the center of Rome in AD 283 initiated the reconstruction of monumental areas like Caesar's Forum, the Curia and the Theater of Pompey. Diocletian was linked to another monumental structure: the complex of baths named after him, the biggest ever built. Apart from several works ordered by Massentius (a circus and a basilica) – later terminated by Constantine, who also began construction of another baths complex – any subsequent building or urban planning activity involved only conservation and restoration of the old monuments, not least of all because the emperors' interest had shifted to the new capital, Constantinople.

164 top - The remains of the Basilica of Massentius, show three covered cross-over naves with vaulted ceilings "a cassonetto" covered in stucco and two rows of arched windows on the walls.

164 bottom - The Baths of Diocletian (298-306 AD) had as their central point the natatio ("swimming pool"). Today, it is part of the Church of Santa Maria degli Angeli which was built to a design by Michelangelo.

164-165 - The Antonian Baths (AD 210-230), better known as the Baths of Caracalla, were the largest ones in the Roman world. From its original structure, we see (on the left and right) the remains of its apsidal rooms with diaphragm niches and two symmetrical lateral gymnasiums.

165 right - The Circus of Massentius was built on the Appian Way in AD 310; in the photo, we can see its central spine with its round *metae* (turning points). In the background, we catch a glimpse of the Mausoleum of Romulus built by Massentius for his son.

At the time of Augustus, artworks expressed establishment of Attic models, in particular with a tendency to imitate the Classical style; Roman art was in fact inspired by Greek art of the 5th to 4th century BC, a phase universally known as the "Classical" Period). At that same time, however, a more pragmatic trend became popular for architecture serving civil and public uses, bringing about the design and building of aqueducts, markets, porticoes, fortification, and public baths. The Classical imitation model can also be seen in examples of contemporary pictorial expression, for instance the frescoes that decorate the interior of the House of Livia, where the touch of one of the period's famous masters is evident (probably Ludius or Studius). The same suburban villa gave forth one of the most renowned statues of Augustus, the *Prima Porta Augustus*. The *princeps* is shown in the pose of the Doryphorus by Polykleitos, but he wears armor – a *lorica* (metal breatplate). The *lorica* is decorated with an allegorical reference to the birth of a new era: the same era celebrated

by the "court" poet, Virgil (70-19 BC). The symbolic imagery pays homage to another famous depiction of armor: that worn by Phidias' *Athena Parthenos*, installed in the center of the Parthenon cella. Augustus' statue thus corresponded to a precise political program that linked the actions of the Roman emperor to those of Pericles and Athena in the Classical era.

In the Augustan period, the so-called minor arts extended and became standard production, especially for creation of ornaments like jewelry and cameos. These objects were a seamless typology from the end of the 1st century BC until at least the end of the 1st century AD, as can be seen from the jewelry discovered at Pompeii. The same continuity is encountered in all the artwork produced in the Julio-Claudian dynasty. The integration of architecture and figurative art also continued during the Flavian dynasty's rule. Significant examples are Nero's *Domus Aurea*, the Flavians' Palazzo della Cancelleria, the Coliseum, the *Domus Augustana* and the Arch of Titus.

166-167 - THE FRESCO IN THE GREAT HALL OF THE HOUSE OF LIVIA ON THE PALATINE HILL CALLED *AD GALLINAS ALBAS* IS A UNIQUE REPRESENTATION OF A GARDEN (NATIONAL ROMAN MUSEUM, ROME).

167 LEFT - THE ARMORED STATUE OF HER HUSBAND, OCTAVIAN AUGUSTUS COMES FROM LIVIA'S VILLA. HIS ARMOR IS DECORATED WITH ALLEGORICAL MOTIFS WHICH RECALL THE IDEOLOGY OF HIS REIGN (VATICAN MUSEUMS, ROME).

167 RIGHT - THIS RELIEF, WHICH DECORATES THE ARCH OF TITUS IN ROME, REPRESENTS THE TRIUMPH OF THE EMPEROR WHO IS TRANSPORTING THE SPOILS TAKEN FROM THE TEMPLE OF JERUSALEM.

168 LEFT - ROMAN GOLD
WORK BOASTED OBJECTS OF
GREAT VALUE; THE DIADEM
PENDANT WITH A CHAIN-
INSCRIBED CORNELIAN STONE
WAS MADE USING THE LOOP-
AND-LOOP TECHNIQUE.
IT COMES FROM THE
TOMB OF CREPEREIA
TRYPHAENA (CAPITOLINE
MUSEUMS, ROME).

168 BOTTOM RIGHT - THE "GEMMA AUGUSTEA",
IS A CAMEO IN ONYX, REPRESENTING THE
CELEBRATION OF AUGUSTUS AND THE MILITARY
VICTORIES OF TIBERIUS (KUNSTHISTORISCHES
MUSEUM, VIENNA).

169 - THIS CAMEO IN SARDONYX REPRESENTS
THE APOTHEOSIS OF EMPEROR CLAUDIUS
(BIBLIOTHÈQUE NATIONALE DE FRANCE, PARIS).

168 TOP RIGHT - ORNAMENTAL
RINGS, DIFFERENT FROM THOSE
USED AS SEALS AND FROM IRON
ENGAGEMENT RINGS, WERE
PRODUCED IN THE ROMAN
WORLD AND USUALLY
CHARACTERIZED BY INSCRIBED
GEMS MOUNTED IN A FIXED

COLLET. IN THESE TWO
EXAMPLES IN GOLD, THE MOST
IMPORTANT GEM IS THE
CORNELIAN INSCRIBED TO
REPRESENT MYTHOLOGICAL
SCENES: A BACCHANTE AND A
HERCULES GRASPING DEIANIRA
(CAPITOLINE MUSEUMS, ROME).

170 top - This gold diadem, found in Egypt and datable to Hadrian's reign presents the figure of the syncretic God Serapis (Zeus, Osiris and Apis) inside a shrine (Egyptian Museum, Cairo).

170 - Seventy-two gold pieces decorate this breast-plate. All the pendants are in the shape of a shrine with, inside, the bull Apis, an animal sacred to Serapis (Egyptian Museum, Cairo).

171 - The ribbon-like necklace from Pompeii (1st century BC) with oval collets, mother-of-pearl inserts and emerald prisms shows the popularity of the combination of these two stones with the Romans (National Archaeological Museum, Naples).

171 center - The shape of the bracelet (*armilla*) most commonly used was that of a snake wound in a spiral; it derives from a Greek prototype, very different from the Etruscan ribbon models. This one comes from Pompeii (1st century BC) (National Archaeological Museum, Naples).

172 - This medallion with cameo in onyx represents a Gorgon and bears witness to the diffusion of this kind of ornamental gem and the glyptic production of the Roman imperial world (Capitoline Museums, Rome).

173 - The two medallions with cut gems show two different iconographic scenes: one shows a priestess making an offering to a statue of Apollo, the other is a portrait of a noblewoman with her hair parted in the middle and a low chignon on her nape; this indicates that the period was the early imperial one (Capitoline Museums, Rome).

174 - This statue of Ulysses was part of the famous statuary group, the marble Odyssey, which decorated the grotto of Tiberius' villa in Sperlonga; it is the work of Rhodes sculptors Agesander, Atanadarus, Polydorus, the same ones as for the Laocoön (3rd century BC) (National Archaeological Museum, Naples).

175 - The "Dying Gaul" is a Roman copy in marble of a Hellenistic original in bronze (220-210 BC) and is from the memorial which Attalus I king of Pergamon erected after his victories over the populations of Celtic origin (Capitoline Museums, Rome).

176 – The face of this drunken faun bears witness to the importance which the cult of Dionysus had in the Roman world (Capitoline Museums, Rome).

177 – The Hellenistic prototype of the dancing satyr is clearly seen in this small statue of a bearded one, with the classic attributes of this iconographic type (National Archaeological Museum, Naples).

The Neo-Attic trend began to abate and then disappeared from figurative expression, replaced by solutions that preferred a spatial perspective linked to plasticity, as can be seen in the admirable triumphal procession on the Arch of Titus. A series of solutions compromising realism and Hellenism were used in painting and in mosaics, in particular in the colored *emblemata* (inlay or mosaic work), in black and white two-tone production, in bas-reliefs or in Pompeian murals.

Conversely, in the field of architecture, *utilitas* (functionality) continued to have the upper hand and the approach was upheld after Trajan's death by his successor Hadrian, in particular with the construction of the Pantheon's new cupola, the building of a temple of Venus in Rome, and creation of his wonderful museum-type villa at Tivoli. The villa, moreover, was the definitive move to dwellings organized on more than one floor, enhanced by complementary structures in the complex that included nymphaea, peristyles and baths. Hadrian's great house-museum at Tivoli served as the scenario for the period's artistic trends, with the prevalence of the style that paid homage to the Classical period of Greek art, but here in terms of reproducing copies. The villa's sculpture collection was modeled, in this same perspective, around the emperor's favorite, his beloved Antinous. During this time, the tendency to mix sculpture and painting styles became popular in the figurative arts, and this was expressed by the use of chiaroscuro, finely represented in the Antonine period (AD 134-192) in the Antonine Column reliefs and in the portraits of the emperors Lucius Verus and Commodus.

A new school of sculpture was also founded at that time, in Ephesus, which circulated its artistic principles in many important towns in the Eastern provinces (e.g., Petra, Palmyra, Baalbek). The Ephesus school marked the breaking point between realism and naturalism, embracing the use of allegory and illusion. The earliest example of this new style is the illustration of the rain miracle, decorating one of the Marcus Aurelius (AD 160-193) column reliefs, erected by his successor, Commodus, to commemorate the campaigns against the German tribes – the Marcomanni and Sarmatians. The style of the Antonine Column, not far from the site of the *ustrinum* (the emperor's funeral pyre), and linked ideologically to Trajan's Column, expressed the irrationalistic sense of events and the existential anguish that typified the closing historic phase of the empire. Technically, the effect was achieved by use of a spiral drill, with a continuous groove or close-set bores, that created an illusionary view of distant surfaces by the impression of a chiaroscuro.

178 - THE PORTRAIT-BUST OF LUCIUS VERUS IS FROM A UNIFORMED PROTOTYPE IN THE CONTEXT OF OFFICIAL PORTRAITURE. IN THIS EXEMPLARY THE USE OF THE METAL-POINTED DRILL HIGHLIGHTS THE VOLUME OF THE HAIRDO WITH PICTORIAL EFFECTS (CAPITOLINE MUSEUMS, ROME).

179 - ANTINOUS, A FAVORITE OF HADRIAN'S, BECOME AN OBJECT OF WORSHIP AFTER HIS DEATH (AD 130) AND BROUGHT TO LIFE A SPECIFIC CLASS OF PORTRAITURE. HERE IS ONE OF THE MOST FAMOUS STATUES REFLECTING THE CLASSIC TENETS FOR HEROIC STATUES (NATIONAL ARCHAEOLOGICAL MUSEUM, NAPLES).

180 - THIS DETAIL SHOWS A ROMAN COPY OF AN HELLENISTIC ORIGINAL OF A SLEEPING HERMAPHRODITE FROM THE FIRST HALF OF THE 2ND CENTURY BC (NATIONAL ROMAN MUSEUM, ROME).

180 - THIS DETAIL SHOWS A ROMAN COPY OF AN HELLENISTIC ORIGINAL OF A SLEEPING HERMAPHRODITE FROM THE FIRST HALF OF THE 2ND CENTURY BC (NATIONAL ROMAN MUSEUM, ROME).

181 - THE STATUE KNOWN AS THE "ESQUILINE" VENUS HAS BEEN RECENTLY RECOGNIZED TO BE OF CLEOPATRA, QUEEN OF EGYPT, ON THE BASIS OF ITS DISTINCT FACIAL FEATURES, NOSE AND SHORT HEIGHT (CAPITOLINE MUSEUMS, ROME).

The historic relief type of sculpture came into vogue at the time of Septimius Severus. There are examples on the Arch of Septimius Severus, at the Roman Forum, and on the Leptis Magna Arch, the town where the emperor was born. Unlike other monuments from the past (for instance the Arch of Titus or the Arch of Trajan in Beneventum (Benevento), where the narration was inspired by celebratory motifs, in this case the artistic expression is in an in epic-dramatic key and centers on the emperor's deeds. These allegorical and illusionary trends were also to be seen in painting and mosaic, especially in portraits that were created using the encaustic technique as in the case of the sarcophagi enclosing the Faiyum mummies, or floor mosaics in Libyan and Sicilian villas. As far as tomb sculpture is concerned, apart from the widespread use of marble sarcophagi, there were figurative themes whose motifs referred to the legend of Dionysus or where civil themes were prevalent, to the detriment of traditional mythological subjects. Scenes also appeared alluding to or promoting the diffusion of the new religion: Christianity.

Monumental art continued to appear in Rome, as in the case of the Baths of Caracalla, but Diocletian's tetrarchic reform of the empire (AD 290) brought the final examples of expressive, productive Roman art, to be seen in the Baths of Diocletian in Rome, his palace in Split, and the Arch of Galerius at Thessalonica.

The 4th century AD, including the reigns of Constantine and Theodosius, may be considered the final fertile period for Roman art. A number of historic circumstances such the administrative centralization and the military pressure against the empire, combined with the economic and social crisis, also seemed to be reflected in the choice of artistic and figurative themes. In fact, a trend was established in which forms were geometrized, accompanied by an eclecticism that associated different styles, including the use of pieces brought from older monuments. For instance, the Trajan reliefs and Hadrian tondoes reutilized in the Arch of Constantine, following a precise political program associated with a totally new figurative language that ignored all precepts of the Classical tradition, especially perspective. Rampant Germanism and the diffusion of Christianity contributed to the further establishment of this eclectic figurative language, which emphasized depiction of imperial majesty in a hieratic sense, combined with the celebration of deeds and allusion to tradition, but expressed according to the principles of a different representation of art, which preceded Byzantinism and heralded the first examples of Medieval art.

182 LEFT - THESE FUNERARY PORTRAITS OF TWO BROTHERS FROM THE FAIYUM, MADE WITH TEMPERA PAINT ON WOOD USING THE ENCAUSTIC TECHNIQUE, COME FROM THE 2ND CENTURY AND RECALL POMPEIAN EXAMPLES FROM THE 1ST CENTURY (EGYPTIAN MUSEUM, CAIRO).

182 RIGHT - THE ARCH OF COSTANTINE BEGAN A NEW FIGURATIVE LANGUAGE AND RE-USED PARTS OF EARLIER MONUMENTS FOR PROPAGANDISTIC AIMS. ON THE FRONT, WE SEE BAS-RELIEFS AND STATUES FROM TRAJAN AND HADRIAN'S ERAS.

183 - THE WINGED VICTORY (*NIKE*) IS ADORNED WITH TASSELS FROM THE ARCH OF SEPTIMIUS SEVERUS IN LEPTIS MAGNA (AD 203-204); ITS VOLUMES ARE HIGHLIGHTED BY THE USE OF A HELICOIDAL DRILL TO UNDERLINE THE PICTORIAL EFFECT (TRIPOLI MUSEUM).

184-185 - The mosaic floor of African workmanship was made using a dual technique: mosaic for the seasonal allegories and the hunting and fishing scenes, while *opus sectile* for the accessory motifs (Tripoli Museum).

186 - THE HEAD OF THE GOD OCEANUS
IN A HEXAGONAL FRAME WITH A BRAID
AROUND IT WAS PART OF THE MOSAIC
DECORATIONS OF THE SABRATHA BATHS;
THE GOD HAS A GARLAND OF FRUIT
AROUND HIS HEAD (SABRATHA MUSEUM).

187 - THIS POLYCHROME ROUND MOSAIC
WAS AT THE CENTER OF A FLOOR
IN THE SABRATHA HOME OF LIBER
PATER; IT DEPICTS A LION'S HEAD
SURROUNDED BY A BRAID MOTIF
(SABRATHA MUSEUM).

188-189 - THIS DETAIL, WHICH
DEPICTS A CALF ASSAULTED BY A
TIGER, IS FROM THE BASILICA OF
JUNIUS BASSUS IN ROME
(AD 331) AND IS MADE OF MARBLE
AND HARD STONE ACCORDING TO
THE *OPUS SECTILE* TECHNIQUE
WITH INLAYS (CAPITOLINE
MUSEUMS, ROME).

190 - The fresco on the wall of the *TABLINUM* of the House of Lucretius Fronto in Pompeii is a good example of the 3rd style (ornamental).

190-191 - This 4th Style (fantastic) *PINAX* is from a wall in the House of the Vettii and portrays the torment of Ixion, tied to a wheel with snakes.

The Pompeii frescoes which decorated both homes and public buildings are almost the only documentation of more than a century and a half of production: from the end of the 2nd century BC up to the volcanic eruption in AD 79. These frescoes also reflect the megalography of Greek painting. In this period we also see a phenomenon which overturns the tenets for building decoration: the renaissance of mural painting, a former Hellenistic tradition. The new works faithfully reflect the prototypes of Greek portraiture, often lost to us. Wall paintings reproducing architectural scenes or landscapes were classified into "styles" of Pompeii painting according to chronology and type. The first style (encrustation), from the 2nd century BC, is characterized by imitations of marble or alabaster in painted stucco and is found, for example, in the House of the Faun in Pompeii. The second style (architectural) became popular in the 1st century BC and refers to scenes (of theater or nature) in perspective which are framed in panels placed between architectural elements. Celebrated examples of this style are seen in Livia's Villa of Prima Porta in Rome, in the Villa of Mysteries in Pompeii and in the Fannius Synistor at Boscoreale. The third style (ornamental) became popular between the mid 1st century BC and the 1st century AD. Here, faux architecture becomes ornamental even though some elements of the previous style, such as a central square wall panel, remain. The fourth and last style (fantastic) was popular from the mid 1st century AD to AD 79. It involves heavy wall embellishment often including fantastic themes and portions in relief in gilded stucco. The most famous examples of this style are seen in the *Domus Aurea* in Rome, the House of Vettii in Pompeii and the House of Lovers also in Pompeii.

192 - The Eros theme is a common one is some 4th style frescoes and in the Hall of Cupids in the House of the Vettii in Pompeii we also see *psychai* (souls) collecting flower petals.

194

194 TOP - THIS DETAIL SHOWS
A STATUETTE OF A WINGED
CUPID, LINKED TO THE RITUAL
WHICH INSPIRED THE NAME
OF THE VILLA OF THE
MYSTERIES IN POMPEII.

194 BOTTOM - THIS SCENE
IS FROM THE LARGE FRIEZE
IN THE VILLA OF THE
MYSTERIES. IT SHOWS A SATYR
OFFERING DRINK TO A YOUTH.
THE PRESENCE OF THIS SCENE
COMBINED WITH THAT OF
A SATYR MASK, MAY DENOTE
A LINK WITH DIONYSIAN
MYSTERY RITES.

195 - THIS CELEBRATED
FLAGELLATION SCENE,
REPRESENTING AN INITIATION
RITE OF THE MYSTERIES,
IS FOUND IN THE MAIN HALL
OF THE VILLA OF THE
MYSTERIES IN POMPEII
(MID 1ST CENTURY BC).

196 - Representations of gardens with doves drinking, inspired by Hellenistic motifs, are seen in Pompeian paintings beginning from the 2nd style. In the House of the Vettii, in Pompeii, these details are joined by a recovery of the still lifes with fowl theme which is also seen in Herculaneum and, especially, in Livia's Villa at Prima Porta, Rome.

197 - The peristyle of the House of Venus in the Sea-shell in Pompeii holds paintings portraying gardens with birds which testify to the popularity of Hellenistic-inspired naturalistic themes.

198 - THE MOSAIC PORTRAYING
DIONYSUS AS A BABE DRINKING
FROM A *KANTHAROS* AND RIDING
A TIGER (HOUSE OF THE FAUN,
POMPEII) IS A HELLENISTIC
MOTIF. THIS ONE IS EMBELLISHED
WITH A FRAME OF GREENERY
AND THEATRICAL MASKS
(NATIONAL ARCHAEOLOGICAL
MUSEUM, NAPLES).

199 - THE HELLENISTIC STILL LIFE
THEME OF DOVES DRINKING FROM
A BASIN ON A THREE-LEGGED
STAND WITH "LEGS" IN THE SHAPE
OF FELINE PAWS WAS INVENTED BY
THE ARTIST SOSOS OF PERGAMUM
AND ALSO APPEARS IN A MOSAIC IN
THE HOUSE OF THE FAUN
(NATIONAL ARCHAEOLOGICAL
MUSEUM, NAPLES).

200 - This mosaic, inserted
in a rhomboidal panel
framed in marble,
depicts a still life
scene with a rooster
"courting" a hen
(National Archaeological
Museum, Naples).

201 - Alexandrian realism
is reflected in the still lifes
in the mosaics of the House
of the Faun: a cat eats
a fowl and, in the lower
register, ducks, fish
and shells appear
(National Archaeological
Museum, Naples).

This brief excursus on Roman civilization has considered a number of historic aspects, as well as some of the more salient and typifying traits of urban planning, not to mention artistic production. It is not difficult to deduce how significant and innovative Rome's accomplishments were, also in the context of religion and organization of a complex military machine, which in the Western World, from the Middle Ages to the present day, have been two privileged channels for merging civic life.

Religious continuity is possibly the most evident heritage of Roman civilization: a large part of religious terminology in use in the Western World is borrowed from Latin vocabulary: *religio* is only the most clear-cut example. Above all, however, the Roman world was a medium that spread Christian doctrine, which acquired an organized status during the closing stages of the empire, which also handed its down to Slavic and Germanic populations. As the destinies of West and East separated, following Diocletian's division of the empire, secular and religious power remained, although there was one difference. Spiritual power in the Byzantine empire continued to be linked to political power, whereas in the West, papal authority was always independent and disengaged from the emperor's "lay" power. This was a detail that defined a differentiation between the Catholic Church (Western) and the Orthodox Church (Eastern). Then, as far as the "universal" aspects were concerned, the Western Church was typified by its use of Latin, whereas in the East, it was increasingly common to use the vulgate.

The empire's concept of heritage is certainly connected to the notion of universal diffusion, and this was a point of reference for power legitimization for a succession of French and German sovereigns, and for Russian rulers in the East.

Another fundamental legacy was linked to urban planning, architecture and engineering, developed by the genius of the Roman workforce. The layout of towns in the Roman urban model and, in particular, the diffusion of the urban-planning scheme that envisaged a center typically divided into different spaces for public life (the forum with annexed buildings) and private life (*domus* and *villae*, entertainment complexes – theaters, amphitheaters, baths), were to be found not only in the newly-acquired towns, but were also present in those with a distinct historical substratum. The centers of many modern cities prove continuity of habitation, despite subsequent overlays, revealing an urban layout and fabric defined in the Roman era, at the time of their acquisition. As far as engineering was concerned, the use of a number of building techniques or of special materials (such as vaults or arches, for instance, or brick), and especially prevalent works of public and functional interest (such as aqueducts or bridges) were an important legacy of Roman civilization. It is still possible to see architectural works, built by the Romans, which have survived the passage of time, and have been brought back into use in the form and for the function they had offered in ancient times.

Of course, other civic and cultural heritage left by Rome includes the institution of a legal system, whose canons were defined in the time of Augustus, and definitively codified in AD 534, during Justinian's reign (AD 527-565). In the field of literary and artistic culture, the contribution of Roman civilization followed on from the Greek model, even if the Roman model succeeded in evolving an original synthesis of values of form and content. Latin literary texts were handed down by the Western Church to the Medieval world as a classical heritage, then completed by the addition of Greek literature, which was preserved by the Byzantine East. This complex operation found its most complete fulfillment in the Renaissance, however, when the Roman legacy contributed to the foundation of an entire heritage of politics, language, philosophy, architecture, literature and figurative arts, which to this day survive in Europe and in the culture of the Western World.

202 - THIS PALEO-CHRISTIAN MOSAIC FROM THE 5TH CENTURY SHOWS A BASILICA WITH TWO TOWERS (THE LOUVRE, PARIS).

203 - THE "BARBERINI DIPTYCH" IN IVORY PORTRAYS A TRIUMPHANT EMPEROR ON HORSEBACK, PROBABLY JUSTINIAN (THE LOUVRE, PARIS).

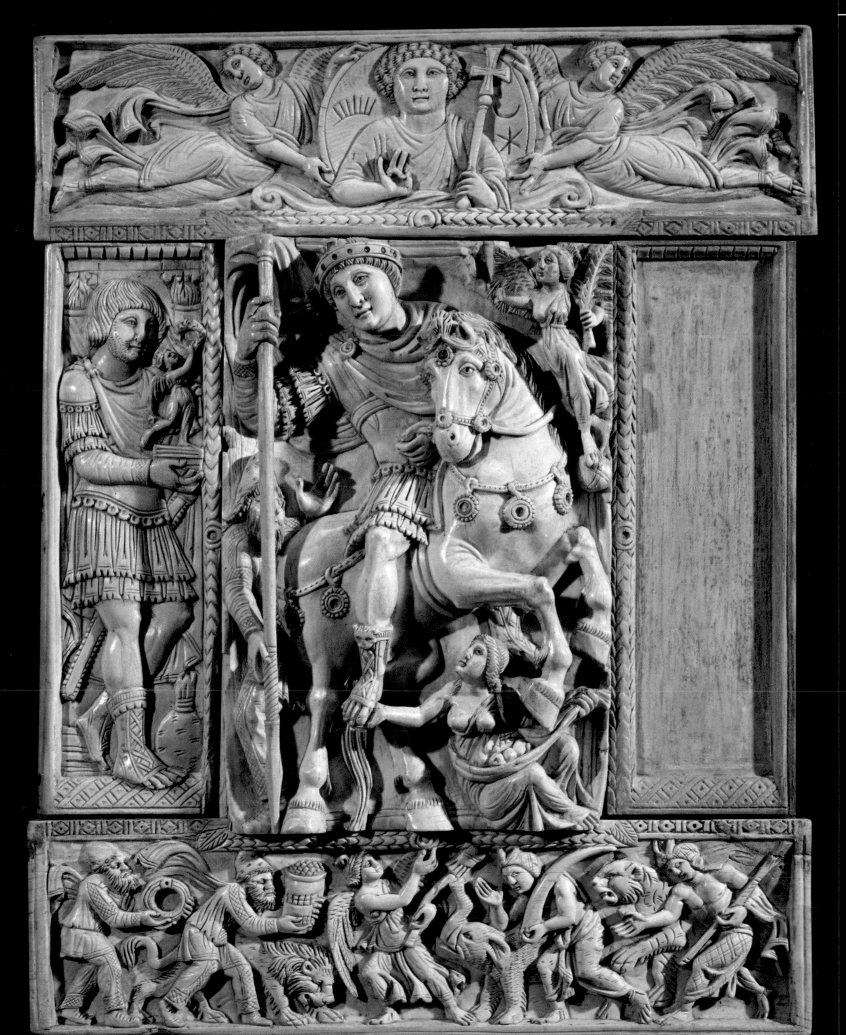

HISTORY AND TREASURES OF AN ANCIENT CIVILIZATION

BIBLIOGRAPHY

R. Bianchi Bandinelli, *Roma. L'arte romana nel centro del potere*, Rizzoli, Milan 1976

R. Bianchi Bandinelli, *Roma e la fine dell'arte antica*, Rizzoli, Milan 1976

G.A. Mansuelli, *Roma e il mondo romano*, 2 voll., UTET, Turin 1981

Roma e l'Italia, radices imperii, Garzanti-Scheiwiller, Milan 1990

S. Settis (edited by), *Civiltà dei Romani*, 4 voll., Electa, Milan 1990

A. Momigliano, A. Schiavone, A. Giardina (edited by), *Storia di Roma*, 8 voll. Einaudi, Turin 1999

PHOTO CREDITS

208 – THE ACRONYM MAY MEAN "THE SENATE AND THE ROMAN PEOPLE" (*SENATUS POPULUSQUE ROMANUS*) OR "THE SENATE AND THE ROMAN PEOPLE OF THE QUIRITES" (*SENATUS POPULUS QUIRITIUM ROMANUS*).